JOSHUA 24:15

And if it seem evil unto you to serve the LORD, choose you this day whom ye will serve; whether the gods which your fathers served that were on the other side of the flood, or the gods of the Amorites, in whose land ye dwell: **but as for me and my house, we will serve the LORD.**

JESUS CHURCH

ESTABLISH – AD 33

JERUSALEM

CAN YOU IDENTIFY YOUR CHURCH IN THE BIBLE

AUTHOR: Johnnie Lee Harris

Copyright 2015 – Johnnie Lee Harris

1-2551377531

*Note: All verses of scriptures quoted in this book are taken from the King James Version of the Holy Bible.

If you do not like reading the KJV of Bible.

I encourage you take a look at the – ASV, ESV, NKJV.

CONTENTS

ACKNOWLEDGEMENTS

INTRODUCTION

PREFACE

CHAPTERS

    1. Scriptures To Consider.................................. 1
    2. Saul, the man call Paul....................................... 27
    3. Jesus.. 38
    4. Patriarchal Age... 42
    5. Mosaic Age.. 51
    6. Christian Age... 56

ACKNOWLEDGEMENTS

I have always wanted to write two books before leaving this earth. Thanks to God for everything He has done for me. Particularly for His Son, whom He let die for us all. I thank my wife in her support with all we have accomplished through this union of marriage we have traveled. She is a true help mate and when we come to a milestone in the road, she waits patiently without complaint until I finish. Then she and I continue on down the road of our travel. Thanks to Bro. Workman who lead me to Christ. Also to the many others who have played a very important part in my life. That have made me the person I am today. I thank God for my Christian family, where my wife and I worship.

INTRODUCTION

My family is of the Baptist Religion. The Baptist Religion got its beginning in England 1608. Roger Williams was instrumental in getting it started in America. Providence, RI. – 1639. Although I was made to go to Sunday school as a child. I never was indoctrinated into the religion. I was taught to believe in God. This one thing, I learned and accept as a child. I do thank God for that. But when I left my parent's home, I stopped attending church. But 1974 my life changed because of curiosity. I had just bought my first home, when two men befriended me in my new neighborhood. Both were trying to get me to attend church with them. At that point in my life I did not know anything about God's word. One day I asked my insurance agent a question, a man of my same age. Why are these two religious men, one being a Muslim and the other Baptist, both trying to get me to go to church with them? They could not agree on what was written in God's word. He did not answer my question, but answer me with a question. Can I have a Bible study with you? So on June 24, 1974 the Bible study came into play. I was taught the – Gospel. After the study, I was asked if I was interested in being baptized for the remission of my sins. My reply was, yes I want to be baptized to get rid of my sins. They took me to the church building, that same night and baptize me. Before the person baptized me he took my confession.

Do you believe Jesus is the Son of God? This confession brought death to our lord Jesus Christ, but it promise to bring life unto you after you have completed your obedience in water baptism for remission of your sins. You arise in newness of life, being faithful until death.

They baptized me that night because they knew the next minute or hour in a persons, life is not promise to you. They knew if I died in my sins I could never make heaven my home. Baptism is a spiritual birth.

*Listen to what Jesus said to a man name Nicodemus.

John 3:1-7

The same came to Jesus by night, and said unto him, Rabbi, we know that thou art a teacher come from God: for no man can do these miracles that thou doest, except God be with him.Jesus answered and said unto him, Verily, verily, I say unto thee, Except a man be born again, he cannot see the kingdom of God. Nicodemus saith unto him, How can a man be born when he is old? can he enter the second time into his mother's womb, and be born?Jesus answered, Verily, verily, I say unto thee, Except a man be born of water and of the Spirit, he cannot enter into the kingdom of God. That which is born of the flesh is flesh; and that which is born of the Spirit is spirit. Marvel not that I said unto thee, Ye must be born again.

PREFACE

Hell is real, but everybody is not going to Heaven. Only those who practice what is in God's word, the Bible. I know there are going to be a lot of controversy about this book, but God's word will prevail.

I am a Priest, and have done everything in God's word to be called a Priest, if I so desire, but that not my aim. I just want to prove a point. When we accepts God's word, we all become Priests.

1Peter 2:5

Ye also, as lively stones, are built up a spiritual house, an holy priesthood, to offer up spiritual sacrifices, acceptable to God.

*Listen to what Jesus said to some religious folk.

Matthew 7:21-23

Not every one that saith unto me, Lord, Lord, shall enter into the kingdom of heaven; but he that doeth the will of my Father which is in heaven. Many will say to me in that day, Lord, Lord, have we not prophesied in thy name? and in thy name have cast out devils? and in thy name done many wonderful works? And then will I profess unto them, I never knew you: depart from me, ye that work iniquity.

*Jesus also said there be few people that will fine – Eternal Life.

Matthew 7:13-14

Enter ye in at the strait gate: for wide is the gate, and broad is the way, that leadeth to destruction, and many there be which go in thereat: Because strait is the gate, and narrow is the way, which leadeth unto life, and few there be that find it.

*Paul makes an alarming point to Israel that applies to some of us today.

Roman 10:1-3

Brethren, my heart's desire and prayer to God for Israel is, that they might be saved.For I bear them record that they have a zeal of God, but not according to knowledge. For they being ignorant of God's righteousness, and going about to establish their own righteousness, have not submitted themselves unto the righteousness of God.

CHAPTER 1

Scriptures to Consider

Look over these scripture and evaluate yourself. I want you to be honest with yourself. We never should rely on others for our salvation. When we stand before God at the judgment we will be standing alone. I am giving you scripture because I do not want to give you my opinion. God's word will never change, but if you do not agree with a scripture, put an "X" by the scripture and you can come back to it when you have finished the book. These scriptures I am sharing with you will help you understand Jesus Church in the Bible. When we get to it.

CAN YOU IDENTIFY YOUR CHURCH IN THE BIBLE

Jesus adds you to His Church

Acts 2:47

Praising God, and having favour with all the people. And the Lord added to the church daily such as should be saved.

*Many people think there is no need to attend worship service. But if you notice the Lord adds the saved to the – Church. Also you do not join the Lord's Church. What you join, you can unjoin. Join comes from the doctrine of men. There are five things one most participate in each Lord's Day – Sunday. The Lord's Supper, preaching, praying, singing, and giving. Some denominations, doctrine of men, take the Lord's Supper once a month or once a year.

Communion / Lord Supper

Acts 20:7

And upon the first day of the week, when the disciples came together to break bread, Paul preached unto them, ready to depart on the morrow; and continued his speech until midnight.

*Notice the disciples of Paul's day took the Lord's Supper on the first day of the week – Sunday.

Church Offering

1Corinthians 16:1-2

Now concerning the collection for the saints, as I have given order to the churches of Galatia, even so do ye. Upon the first day of the week let every one of you lay by him in store, as God hath prospered him, that there be no gatherings when I come.

*We see here they collected money on the first of the week as well. Than why do some Church of today take up the offering, but neglect to take part in the Lord's Supper on the first day of the week?

Church Assemble

Hebrews 10:25-26

Not forsaking the assembling of ourselves together, as the manner of some is; but exhorting one another: and so much the more, as ye see the day approaching. For if we sin wilfully after that we have received the knowledge of the truth, there remaineth no more sacrifice for sins,

*Once we have obeyed God's word and then we refuse to assemble with His people that is a sin. The Church assembles on the first day of the week – Sunday.

THE BIBLE

2Timothy 3:16-17

All scripture is given by inspiration of God, and is profitable for doctrine, for reproof, for correction, for instruction in righteousness: That the man of God may be perfect, thoroughly furnished unto all good works.

*All scripture / The Bible is God's word to mankind.

Genesis 1:26

And God said, Let us make man in our image, after our likeness: and let them have dominion over the fish of the sea, and over the fowl of the air, and over the cattle, and over all the earth, and over every creeping thing that creepeth upon the earth.

*Have you ever noticed in all God made, mankind is the only one He gave a manual to fix himself. Still very few people take the time to study The Bible.

1Thessalonians 4:11

And that ye study to be quiet, and to do your own business, and to work with your own hands, as we commanded you;

1Timothy 2:15

Study to shew thyself approved unto God, a workman that needeth not to be ashamed, rightly dividing the word of truth.

*If you can rightly divide the Bible, you can wrongfully divide it as well.

Jesus Baptism

Matthew 3:11-16

I indeed baptize you with water unto repentance. but he that cometh after me is mightier than I, whose shoes I am not worthy to bear: he shall baptize you with the Holy Ghost, and with fire: Whose fan is in his hand, and he will throughly purge his floor, and gather his wheat into the garner; but he will burn up the chaff with unquenchable fire. Then cometh Jesus from Galilee to Jordan unto John, to be baptized of him. But John forbad him, saying, I have need to be baptized of thee, and comest thou to me? And Jesus answering said unto him, **Suffer it to be so now:** for thus it **becometh us to fulfil all righteousness.** Then he suffered him. And Jesus, when he was baptized, went up straightway out of the water: and, lo, the heavens were opened unto him, **and he saw the Spirit of God descending like a dove,** and lighting upon him:

*Jesus replies to John. Suffer it to be so now. For thus it becometh us to fulfil all righteousness. Jesus had no sins, but made a statement in baptism that we should follow in His steps. **He was given the Holy Spirit at that moment of His Baptism. We receive the Holy Spirit after our Baptism as well. Take notice of the scriptures below.**

*Some teach baptism is not essential. But take notice to what Jesus said.

Mark 16: 15-16

And he said unto them, Go ye into all the world, and preach the gospel to every creature. He that believeth and is baptized shall be saved; but he that believeth not shall be damned.

*Jesus said we are saved after - Baptism.

Romans 6:3-7

Know ye not, that so many of us as were baptized into Jesus Christ were baptized into his death? Therefore we are buried with him by baptism into death: that like as Christ was raised up from the dead by the glory of the Father, even so we also should walk in newness of life. For if we have been planted together in the likeness of his death, we shall be also in the likeness of his resurrection: Knowing this, that our old man is crucified with him, that the body of sin might be destroyed, that henceforth we should not serve sin. For he that is dead is freed from sin.

*Baptism is a burial in water. Immersion in water.

The Ethiopian, a eunuch of great authority under Candace Queen of the Ethiopians. Take notice of the steps in his conversion to Jesus Christ by Philip.

Acts 8: 26 -38

And the angel of the Lord spake unto Philip, saying, Arise, and go toward the south unto the way that goeth down from Jerusalem unto Gaza, which is desert.And he arose and went: and, behold, a man of Ethiopia, an eunuch of great authority under Candace queen of the Ethiopians, who had the charge of all her treasure, and had come to Jerusalem for to worship, Was returning, and sitting in his chariot read Esaias the prophet. Then the Spirit said unto Philip, Go near, and join thyself to this chariot.And Philip ran thither to him, and heard him read the prophet Esaias, and said, Understandest thou what thou readest? And he said, How can I, except some man should guide me? And he desired Philip that he would come up and sit with him. The place of the scripture which he read was this, He was led as a sheep to the slaughter; and like a lamb dumb before his shearer, so opened he not his mouth: In his humiliation his judgment was taken away: and who shall declare his generation? for his life is taken from the earth. And the eunuch answered Philip, and said, I pray thee, of whom speaketh the prophet this? of himself, or of some other man? Then Philip opened his mouth, and began at the same scripture, and preached unto him Jesus. And as they went on their way, they came unto a certain water: and the eunuch said, See, here is water; what doth hinder me to be baptized? And Philip said, If thou believest with all thine heart, thou mayest. And he answered and said, I believe that Jesus Christ is the Son of God. And he commanded the chariot to stand still: and they went down both into the water, both Philip and the eunuch; and he baptized him. And when they were come up out of the water, the Spirit of the Lord caught away Philip, that the eunuch saw him no more: and he went on his way rejoicing.

*The Bible said Philip preached to him Jesus. Notice Philip said nothing about water. But the eunuch questioned Philip. There is water what doth hinder me to be baptized. This let me know when you teach someone the Gospel, baptism is part of the scenario. Then both went into the water and Philip baptized him. Baptism is a burial - Romans 6:3-4.

The Holy Spirit is given to us at Baptism

1John 4:13

Hereby know we that we dwell in him, and he in us, because he hath given us of his Spirit.

1Corinthians 12:7

But the manifestation of the Spirit is given to every man to profit withal.

Acts 5:32

And we are his witnesses of these things; and so is also the Holy Ghost, whom God hath given to them that obey him.

Acts 2:38

Then Peter said unto them, Repent, and be baptized every one of you in the name of Jesus Christ for the remission of sins, and ye shall receive the gift of the Holy Ghost.

Chapter of Faith

Hebrews 11:1-6

Now faith is the substance of things hoped for, the evidence of things not seen. For by it the elders obtained a good report. Through faith we understand that the worlds were framed by the word of God, so that things which are seen were not made of things which do appear. By faith Abel offered unto God a more excellent sacrifice than Cain, by which he obtained witness that he was righteous, God testifying of his gifts: and by it he being dead yet speaketh. By faith Enoch was translated that he should not see death; and was not found, because God had translated him: for before his translation he had this testimony, that he pleased God. But without faith it is impossible to please him: for he that cometh to God must believe that he is, and that he is a rewarder of them that diligently seek him.

*Dictionary meaning of faith – allegiance, belief and trust in God, confidence, and **system of religious belief.**

Have you ever had someone ask you about your religious faith.

I have come to believe, in a many cases they really do not understand the question they are asking you themselves.

The system of religious belief consist of many different religions. Baptist, Adventist, Methodist, African Methodist, and Episcopal Church etc. Each of these religious beliefs have **their own doctrine**. Do not take my word for what I just said. Check it out with; The World Book Encyclopedia. Most of these religious beliefs in many ways are contrary to the teaching of God's Word.

Adding and taking From God's Word.

Revelation 22:18-19

For I testify unto every man that heareth the words of the prophecy of this book, If any man shall add unto these things, God shall add unto him the plagues that are written in this book: And if any man shall take away from the words of the book of this prophecy, God shall take away his part out of the book of life, and out of the holy city, and from the things which are written in this book.

2Timothy 4:3-4

For the time will come when they will not endure sound doctrine; but after their own lusts shall they heap to themselves teachers, having itching ears; And they shall turn away their ears from the truth, and shall be turned unto fables.

Matthew 15:9

But in vain they do worship me, teaching for doctrines the commandments of men.

Jesus' Doctrine

2John 1:9

Whosoever transgresseth, and abideth not in the doctrine of Christ, hath not God. He that abideth in the doctrine of Christ, he hath both the Father and the Son.

Hebrews 6:2

Of the **doctrine of baptisms**, and of laying on of hands, and of resurrection of the dead, and of eternal judgment.

*Doctrine of Baptism; Jesus' Baptism is what a person takes part in after they accepts the – Gospel. The Gospel is the doctrine of our Lord and Saviour Jesus Christ.

1Corinthians 15:1-4 definition of the Gospel.

Moreover, brethren, I declare unto you the gospel which I preached unto you, which also ye have received, and wherein ye stand; By which also ye are saved, if ye keep in memory what I preached unto you, unless ye have believed in vain. For I delivered unto you first of all that which I also received, how that Christ died for our sins according to the scriptures; And that he was buried, and that he rose again the third day according to the scriptures:

Commands of Jesus

Matthew 28:18-20

And Jesus came and spake unto them, saying, All power is given unto me in heaven and in earth. Go ye therefore, and teach all nations, baptizing them in the name of the Father, and of the Son, and of the Holy Ghost: Teaching them **to observe** all things whatsoever I have commanded you: and, lo, I am with you always, even unto the end of the world. Amen.

*Observe; conform to. Jesus gave a command and we are to observe it.

Mark 16:15-16

And he said unto them, Go ye into all the world, and preach the gospel to every creature. He that believeth and is **baptized shall be saved**; but he that believeth not shall be damned.

*Some statements and questions the Jews had about the doctrine of Jesus Christ.

Mark 11:18

And the scribes and chief priests heard it, and sought how they might destroy him: for they feared him, because all the people was astonished at his doctrine.

John 7:16

Jesus answered them, and said, My doctrine is not mine, but his that sent me.

*God sent Jesus into the world to do His will.

1Timothy 4:16

Take heed unto thyself, and unto the doctrine; continue in them: for in doing this thou shalt both save thyself, and them that hear thee.

*This doctrine is still being taught in the world today.

What Constitutes, A Christian

Acts 26:25-29

And as he thus spake for himself, Festus said with a loud voice, Paul, thou art beside thyself; much learning doth make thee mad. But he said, I am not mad, most noble Festus; but speak forth the words of truth and soberness. For the king knoweth of these things, before whom also I speak freely: for I am persuaded that none of these things are hidden from him; for this thing was not done in a corner.

King Agrippa, believest thou the prophets? I know that thou believest. Then Agrippa said unto Paul, **Almost thou persuadest me to be a Christian.**

*When someone is taught the Gospel of Jesus Christ they become a follower of Jesus. They are called a Christian, because they become a part of the spiritual family of God. It seems as if King Agrippa understood that.

1Peter 4:14-17

If ye be reproached for the name of Christ, happy are ye; for the spirit of glory and of God resteth upon you: on their part he is evil spoken of, but on your part he is glorified. But let none of you suffer as a murderer, or as a thief, or as an evildoer, or as a busybody in other men's matters. **Yet if any man suffer as a Christian,** let him not be ashamed; but let him glorify God on this behalf. For the time is come that judgment must begin at the house of God: and if it first begin at us, what shall the end be of them that obey not the gospel of God?

*If you would go back and take a look at: Acts 8:26-38, after Philip baptized the Ethiopian Eunuch, the Eunuch now can be called a Christian. Because he has obeyed all Jesus expected of Him. There are no Christians in the Bible known as a Baptist Christian, Adventist Christian, Methodist Christian, Episcopal Christian, Lutheran Christian, and Presbyterian Christian etc. These are the doctrine of men and you cannot find them in the - Bible.

*We were born in the United of America. That makes us and American citizen. When we study and stay in the Bible and obey Jesus commands. That makes us a Christian and nothing else.

When it comes to God's word we have to be in one accord.

1Corninthians 1:10

Now I beseech you, brethren, by the name of our Lord Jesus Christ, that ye all speak the same thing, and that there be no divisions among you; but that ye be perfectly joined together in the same mind and in the same judgment.

*Speak the same. The Bible does not tell one group of people one thing and another something else.

2Peter 1:20-21

Knowing this first, that no prophecy of the scripture is of any private interpretation. For the prophecy came not in old time by the will of man: but holy men of God spake as they were moved by the Holy Ghost.

*God, Jesus, and the Holy Spirit will never speak anything contrary of each other. When it comes to reading the Bible it should be the same with us.

1 John 5:7

For there are three that bear **record** in heaven, the Father, the Word, and the Holy Ghost: and these three are one.

*The record of the Father-God, the Word-Jesus, and the Holy Ghost-Holy Spirit will always be the same.

Matthew 16:19

And I will give unto thee the keys of the kingdom of heaven: and whatsoever thou shalt bind on earth shall be bound in heaven: and whatsoever thou shalt loose on earth shall be loosed in heaven.

*If you take notice of this verse, it proves the confirmation of the God Head. Ratify, verify, and obligate the same thing.

John 14: 23-26

Jesus answered and said unto him, If a man love me, he will keep my words: and my Father will love him, and we will come unto him, and make our abode with him. He that loveth me not keepeth not my sayings: and the word which ye hear is not mine, but the Father's which sent me. These things have I spoken unto you, being yet present with you. But the Comforter, which is the Holy Ghost, whom the Father will send in my name, he shall teach you all things, and bring all things to your remembrance, whatsoever I have said unto you.

*If the Godhead is in one accord, where you think our mindset should be when it comes to the Bible. This lets me know when it comes to the Church, we have to teach and believe the same thing. There cannot be any division between us.

The Church and the Kingdom is one and the same.

Colossians 1:13-18

Who hath delivered us from the power of darkness, and hath translated us into **the kingdom of his dear Son:** In whom we have redemption through his blood, even the forgiveness of sins: Who is the image of the invisible God, the firstborn of every creature: For by him were all things created, that are in heaven, and that are in earth, visible and invisible, whether they be thrones, or dominions, or principalities, or powers: all things were created by him, and for him: And he is before all things, and by him all things consist. And he is the **head of the body, the church:** who is the beginning, the firstborn from the dead; that in all things he might have the preeminence.

Matthew 16:18-19

And I say also unto thee, That thou art Peter, and upon this rock I will **build my church**; and the gates of hell shall not prevail against it. And I will give unto thee the keys of **the kingdom of heaven**: and whatsoever thou shalt bind on earth shall be bound in heaven: and whatsoever thou shalt loose on earth shall be loosed in heaven.

Jesus died for the New Testament

Hebrews 9:11-28

But Christ being come an high priest of good things to come, by a greater and more perfect tabernacle, not made with hands, that is to say, not of this building; Neither by the blood of goats and calves, but by his own blood he entered in once into the holy place, having obtained eternal redemption for us. For if the blood of bulls and of goats, and the ashes of an heifer sprinkling the unclean, sanctifieth to the purifying of the flesh: How much more shall the blood of Christ, who through the eternal Spirit offered himself without spot to God, purge your conscience from dead works to serve the living God? And for this cause he is the mediator of the new testament, that by means of death, for the redemption of the transgressions that were under the first testament, they which are called might receive the promise of eternal inheritance. For where a testament is, there must also of necessity be the death of the testator. For a testament is of force after men are dead: otherwise it is of no strength at all while the testator liveth. Whereupon neither the first testament was dedicated without blood. For when Moses had spoken every precept to all the people according to the law, he took the blood of calves and of goats, with water, and scarlet wool, and hyssop, and sprinkled both the book, and all the people, Saying, This is the blood of the testament which God hath enjoined unto you. Moreover he sprinkled with blood both the tabernacle, and all the vessels of the ministry. And almost all things are by the law purged with blood;

and without shedding of blood is no remission. It was therefore necessary that the patterns of things in the heavens should be purified with these; but the heavenly things themselves with better sacrifices than these. For Christ is not entered into the holy places made with hands, which are the figures of the true; but into heaven itself, now to appear in the presence of God for us: Nor yet that he should offer himself often, as the high priest entereth into the holy place every year with blood of others; For then must he often have suffered since the foundation of the world: but now once in the end of the world hath he appeared to put away sin by the sacrifice of himself. **And as it is appointed unto men once to die, but after this the judgment:** So Christ was once offered to bear the sins of many; and unto them that look for him shall he appear the second time without sin unto salvation.

Hebrews 7:22

By so much was Jesus made a surety of a better testament.

*The Bible consists of Two Testaments. But both are not for mankind to live by today. When Jesus arose from the dead, He bought in The New Testament. The purpose of the Old Testament, listen at what Paul said of the Old Testament.

Romans 15:4

For whatsoever things were written aforetime were written for our learning, that we through patience and comfort of the scriptures might have hope.

*Listen to what Jesus said in The New Testament.

Matthew 26:28

For this is my blood of the new testament, which is shed for many for the remission of sins.

Mark 14:22-24

And as they did eat, Jesus took bread, and blessed, and brake it, and gave to them, and said, Take, eat: this is my body. And he took the cup, and when he had given thanks, he gave it to them: and they all drank of it. And he said unto them, This is my blood of the new testament, which is shed for many.

2Corinthians 3:6

Who also hath made us able ministers of the new testament; not of the letter, but of the spirit: for the letter killeth, but the spirit giveth life.

*But still many religious groups and doctrine of men try to justify what they practice with the Old Testament.

Instrumental Music, should not be part of the worship service.

Psalms 150:1-6

Praise ye the LORD. Praise God in his sanctuary: praise him in the firmament of his power. Praise him for his mighty acts: praise him according to his excellent greatness. Praise him with the sound of the trumpet: praise him with the psaltery and harp. Praise him with the timbrel and dance: praise him with stringed instruments and organs. Praise him upon the loud cymbals: praise him upon the high sounding cymbals. Let every thing that hath breath praise the LORD. Praise ye the LORD.

PSALMS 100:1-2

Make a joyful noise unto the LORD, all ye lands. Serve the LORD with gladness: come before his presence with singing.

*Many use these scriptures to have instrumental music in their worship service. I just shared with you the scriptures that prove Jesus died for the New Testament Church. So how can a church or any doctrine of men justify having instrumental music in the Church. Jesus never told us to have it in His Church. His Apostles never had it in the Church while they were living. Let us take a look at some words of wisdom where God is speaking of instrumental music in The Old Testament.

Amos 6:1-5

Woe to them that are at ease in Zion, and trust in the mountain of Samaria, which are named chief of the nations, to whom the house of Israel came! Pass ye unto Calneh, and see; and from thence go ye to Hamath the great: then go down to Gath of the Philistines: be they better than these kingdoms? or their border greater than your border? Ye that put far away the evil day, and cause the seat of violence to come near; That lie upon beds of ivory, and stretch themselves upon their couches, and eat the lambs out of the flock, and the calves out of the midst of the stall; That chant to the sound of the viol, and invent to themselves instruments of **musick, like David;**

*woe- grief, affliction or danger.

Amos 5: 21-23

I hate, I despise your feast days, and I will not smell in your solemn assemblies. Though ye offer me burnt offerings and your meat offerings, I will not accept them: neither will I regard the peace offerings of your fat beasts. **Take thou away from me the noise of thy songs; for I will not hear the melody of thy viols.**

Isaiah 5:12

And the harp, and the viol, the tabret, and pipe, and wine, are in their feasts: **but they regard not the work of the LORD**, neither consider the operation of his hands.

*If God did not care for their mechanical instrumental music in The Old Testament, what makes you think God would accept it in The New Testament Church? If you would take a very close look at your Bible you will fine "A'cappela" singing is only accepted in the New Testament Church.

A'cappela – music is specifically group or solo singing without instrumental accompaniment.

Ephesians 5: 19

Speaking to yourselves in psalms and hymns and spiritual songs, singing and making melody in your heart to the Lord;

Colossians 3:16

Let the word of Christ dwell in you richly in all wisdom; teaching and admonishing one another in psalms and hymns and spiritual songs, singing with grace in your hearts to the Lord.

Hebrews 13:15

By him therefore let us offer the sacrifice of praise to God continually, that is, **the fruit of our lips** giving thanks to his name.

*Note: singing, the fruit of our lips.

Tongues, a known Languages they could understand.

Acts 2:1-16

And when the day of Pentecost was fully come, they were all with one accord in one place. And suddenly there came a sound from heaven as of a rushing mighty wind, and it filled all the house where they were sitting. And there appeared unto them cloven tongues like as of fire, and it sat upon each of them. And they were all filled with the Holy Ghost, and began **to speak with other tongues**, as the Spirit gave them utterance. And there were dwelling at Jerusalem Jews, devout men, out of every nation under heaven. Now when this was noised abroad, the multitude came together, and were confounded**, because that every man heard them speak in his own language.** And they were all amazed and marvelled, saying one to another, Behold, are not all these which speak **Galilaeans**? And how hear we every man in our own tongue, wherein we were born? **Parthians**, and **Medes**, and **Elamites**, and the dwellers in **Mesopotamia**, and in **Judaea**, and **Cappadocia**, in **Pontus,** and **Asia, Phrygia**, and **Pamphylia**, in **Egypt**, and in the parts of **Libya** about **Cyrene**, and strangers of **Rome, Jews** and **proselytes, Cretes** and **Arabians**, we do hear them speak in our tongues the wonderful works of God. And they were all amazed, and were in doubt, saying one to another, What meaneth this. Others mocking said, These men are full of new wine. But Peter, standing up with the eleven, lifted up his voice, and said unto them, Ye men of Judaea, and all ye that dwell at Jerusalem, be this known unto you, and hearken to my word: For these are not drunken, as ye suppose, seeing it is but the third hour of the day. But this is that which was spoken by **the prophet Joel;**

*If you would read these scriptures carefully, you will see "tongues or languages" could be understood by each native that heard these men. This was the first time in Bible History of The New Testament this was done. Many read these verses and others reference to it in the Bible, then come up with the idea that they can speak in tongues. God used tongues to confirm His word on earth. After the death of the Apostles and others, tongue speaking came to an end. We have the Bible to supply our every need to know God's will for us. Before the Bible was handed down to mankind. God used many tangible things to get His point or will over to man. In many cases God allowed the theory of nature to be altered to get His meaning across. Remember the parting of the Red Sea, Noah and the flood, the virgin birth, and Jesus raising from dead. All this was done for a reason. There is no different in the Apostles speaking in a language they had never learned.

1Cornthians 14:22

 Wherefore **tongues are for a sign**, not to them that believe, **but to them that believe not**: but prophesying serveth not for them that believe not, **but for them which believe**."

*There is a threefold exploitation of the Holy Spirit why God allowed the Apostles to speak an unlearned language. Remember up to this point in time the Jews were God's people.

*If you notice Paul in "1Cornthians 14:22" he address everything in the verses you just read in Acts 2: 1-16.

1. **But to them that believe not**; Are not all these which speak Galilaeans? And how hear we every man in our own tongue, wherein we were born. These are the unbelievers.

2. **Prophesying is for them that believe**; But this is that which was spoken by the prophet Joel. The Jews were believers, because they knew the scriptures and they knew of Joel.

3. Also **tongue speaking** was a way to show the Jews there is **no respecter of person with God**.

 Acts 10:1-48.

20

*Cornelius was a Gentile, he and his household received the Holy Spirit and spoke in tongues.This was a sign to show the Jews God is no respecter of person.

Acts 10:32-35

Send therefore to Joppa, and call hither Simon, whose surname is Peter; he is lodged in the house of one Simon a tanner by the sea side: who, when he cometh, shall speak unto thee. Immediately therefore I sent to thee; and thou hast well done that thou art come. Now therefore are we all here present before God, to hear all things that are commanded thee of God. Then Peter opened his mouth, and said, Of a truth I perceive that **God is no respecter of persons**: But in every nation he that feareth him, and worketh righteousness, is accepted with him.

Acts 10:44-48 The Gentiles spoke in tongues.

While Peter yet spake these words, the Holy Ghost fell on all them which heard the word. And they of the circumcision which believed were astonished, as many as came with Peter, because that on the Gentiles also was poured out the gift of the Holy Ghost. For they heard them **speak with tongues**, and magnify God. Then answered Peter, Can any man forbid water, that these should not be baptized, which have **received the Holy Ghost as well as we?** And he commanded them to be baptized in the name of the Lord. Then prayed they him to tarry certain days.

*What is the need for us to be able to talk in tongues when we have the Bible? These people did not have the finished word like we have today.

Bible, Gods Word

2Timothy 3:16-17

All scripture is given by inspiration of God, and is profitable for doctrine, for reproof, for correction, for instruction in righteousness: That the man of God may be perfect, thoroughly furnished unto all good works.

Tongues Would End.

1Corinthians 13:8

Charity never faileth: but whether there be prophecies, they shall fail; whether there be tongues, they shall cease; whether there be knowledge, it shall vanish away.

*Tongues will cease and unlearned knowledge will vanish away. We have to be careful not to add or subtract from God's word. God is still the same yesterday as well as today.

Romans 1:28

And even as they did not like to retain God in their knowledge, God gave them over to a **reprobate mind**, to do those things which are not convenient;

Jesus Church, what should it be call

Matthews 16:18

And I say also unto thee, That thou art Peter, and upon this rock I will build my church; and the gates of hell shall not prevail against it.

*Jesus said He was going to build a Church. Would you not think it should wear the name of Jesus? The Church of Christ, Church God and The Church of the living God.

John 3:25-36

Then there arose a question between some of John's disciples and the Jews about purifying. And they came unto John, and said unto him, Rabbi, he that was with thee beyond Jordan, to whom thou barest witness, behold, the same baptizeth, and all men come to him. John answered and said, A man can receive nothing, except it be given him from heaven. Ye yourselves bear me witness, that I said, I am not the Christ, but that I am sent before him. He that hath the bride is the bridegroom: but the friend of the bridegroom, which standeth and heareth him, rejoiceth greatly because of the bridegroom's voice: this my joy therefore is fulfilled. He must increase, but I must decrease. He that cometh from above is above all: he that is of the earth is earthly, and speaketh of the earth: he that cometh from heaven is above all. And what he hath seen and heard, that he testifieth; and no man receiveth his testimony. He that hath received his testimony hath set to his seal that God is true. For he whom God hath sent speaketh the words of God: for **God giveth not the Spirit by measure unto him**. The Father loveth the Son, and **hath given all things into his hand**. He that believeth on the Son hath everlasting life: and he that believeth not the Son shall not see life; but the wrath of God abideth on him.

*The Bride is the Church.

The Mystery of the Church

Ephesians 5:23-32

For the husband is the head of the wife, even as Christ is the head of the church: and he is the saviour of the body. Therefore as the church

23

is subject unto Christ, so let the wives be to their own husbands in every thing. Husbands, love your wives, even as Christ also loved the church, and gave himself for it; That he might sanctify and cleanse it with the washing of water by the word, That he might present it to himself a glorious church, not having spot, or wrinkle, or any such thing; but that it should be holy and without blemish. So ought men to love their wives as their own bodies. He that loveth his wife loveth himself. For no man ever yet hated his own flesh; but nourisheth and cherisheth it, even as the Lord the church: For we are members of his body, of his flesh, and of his bones. For this cause shall a man leave his father and mother, and shall be joined unto his wife, and they two shall be one flesh. This is a great mystery: but I speak concerning Christ and the church.

Ephesians 3:21

Unto him be glory in the church by Christ Jesus throughout all ages, world without end. Amen.

Romans 16:16

Salute one another with an holy kiss. The churches of Christ salute you.

*If Jesus is the owner of the Church and it has His name, it's absolutely necessary we practice His doctrine. Remember, Jesus Doctrine was first preached in Acts 2:1- 47. Take notice verse 47, the Lord added those saved to the Church. Something I believe we need to consider, before we built building to meet in. What was these Church in the house, Christian of the days of old met in called.

Greek definition for Church, originally meant an assembly.

Acts 8:3

As for Saul, he made havock of the church, entering into every house, and haling men and women committed them to prison.

Romans 16:5

 Likewise greet the church that is in their house. Salute my well-beloved Epaenetus, who is the firstfruits of Achaia unto Christ.

Colossians 4:15

Salute the brethren which are in Laodicea, and Nymphas, and the church which is in his house.

Philemon 1:2

And to our beloved Apphia, and Archippus our fellowsoldier, and to the church in thy house:

*The assembly that met in these houses. The Church of Christ, the Church Jesus built. His Church will never cease to exist. You just got to find it. When you have finish this book you will know how to find it. Can you identify your church in the Bible?

*Study for yourself and stay true to God's word. Because when Jesus returns it will be too late to change.

2Peter 3:9-18

 The Lord is not slack concerning his promise, as some men count slackness; but is longsuffering to us-ward, not willing that any should perish, but that all should come to repentance. But the day of the Lord will come as a thief in the night; in the which the heavens shall pass away with a great noise, and the elements shall melt with fervent heat, the earth also and the works that are therein shall be burned up. Seeing then that all these things shall be dissolved, what manner of persons ought ye to be in all holy conversation and godliness, Looking for and hasting unto the coming of the day of God, wherein the heavens being on fire shall be dissolved, and the elements shall melt with fervent heat? Nevertheless we, according to his promise, look for new heavens and a new earth, wherein dwelleth righteousness. Wherefore, beloved, seeing that ye look for such things, be diligent that ye may be found of him in peace, without spot, and blameless. And account that the longsuffering of our Lord is salvation; even as our beloved brother Paul also according to the wisdom given unto him hath **written unto you;** As also in all **his epistles, speaking in them of these things**; in which are **some things hard to be understood**, which **they that are unlearned and unstable wrest**, as they do also the other scriptures, **unto their own destruction.** Ye therefore, beloved, **seeing ye know these things before, beware lest ye also, being led away with the error of the wicked, fall from your own stedfastness.** But grow in grace, and in the **knowledge of our Lord and Saviour Jesus Christ**. To him be glory both now and for ever. Amen

Chapter 2

Saul, the man call Paul

Acts13:9 Then Saul, (who also is called Paul,) filled with the Holy Ghost, set his eyes on him.

*Before Saul got to this point in his life, he tried to end the doctrine of Jesus and get rid of the Lords Church forever. Saul and Jesus both were born under the Mosiac Age, The Law of Moses. Saul knew the Holy Scriptures, and of the Messiah as a King and ruler of David's house. Who should come to earth and restore the kingdom of David. Saul as well as all the Jews thought it would be an earthly kingdom.

*Saul's religious back-ground. Before he was converted to Christianity.

Acts 26:4-5

My manner of life from my youth, which was at the first among mine own nation at Jerusalem, know all the Jews; Which knew me from the beginning, if they would testify, that after the most straitest sect of our religion I lived a Pharisee.

*In the time of Saul, there were two sects of religious groups. The Pharisee and Sadducee and now another one is coming into play Christianity. Saul had a problem with this, because Christianity was going to change the custom of things. Gentiles also were being added to God's people.

Listen at what Saul said after he was converted to Jesus Christianity.

Acts 13:46

Then Paul and Barnabas waxed bold, and said, It was necessary that the word of God should first have been spoken to you: but seeing ye put it from you, and judge yourselves unworthy of everlasting life, lo, we turn to the Gentiles.

Galatians 1:13-14

For ye have heard of my conversation in time past in the Jews' religion, how that beyond measure I persecuted the church of God, and wasted it: And profited in the Jews' religion above many my equals in mine own nation, being more exceedingly zealous of the traditions of my fathers.

*Jesus said His Kingdom is not of this world. Jesus Kingdom is a Spiritual Kingdom, which is the Church.

John 18:33-37

Then Pilate entered into the judgment hall again, and called Jesus, and said unto him, Art thou the King of the Jews? Jesus answered him, Sayest thou this thing of thyself, or did others tell it thee of me? Pilate answered, Am I a Jew? Thine own nation and the chief priests have delivered thee unto me: what hast thou done? Jesus answered, **My kingdom is not of this world: if my kingdom were of this world, then would my servants fight**, that I should not be delivered to the Jews: but now is my kingdom not from hence. Pilate therefore said unto him, Art thou a king then? Jesus answered, Thou sayest that I am a king. To this end was I born, and for this cause came I into the world, that I should bear witness unto the truth. Every one that is of the truth heareth my voice.

*The question, can you identify your church in the Bible? Can the history of your church be traced back to this point in history, before Jesus died for the Church?

Jesus Defense

Matthew 26:59-66

Now the chief priests, and elders, and all the council, sought false witness against Jesus, to put him to death; But found none: yea, though many false witnesses came, yet found they none. At the last came two false witnesses, And said, This fellow said, **I am able to destroy the temple of God, and to build it in three days.** And the high priest arose, and said unto him, Answerest thou nothing? what is it which these witness against thee? But Jesus held his peace, And the high priest answered and said unto him, I adjure thee by the living God, that thou tell us whether thou be the Christ, the Son of God. Jesus saith unto him, Thou hast said: nevertheless I say unto you, Hereafter shall ye see the Son of man sitting on the right hand of power, and coming in the clouds of heaven. Then the high priest rent his clothes, saying, He hath spoken blasphemy; what further need have we of witnesses? behold, now ye have heard his blasphemy. What think ye? They answered and said, He is guilty of death.

*Build it in three days. Jesus said this, but he was talking about his death, burial, and resurrection. After Jesus resurrection, we see the Spiritual Kingdom / Church came into existence in Acts 2:1- 47. The Lord added the saved to the Church. Verse 47.

*Let us take a look at some of the things **Saul did to stop the growth of the Lord's Church**. Early as 606 AD men thru the doctrine of men, have added and taken from the doctrine of Jesus. These doctrine of men is no different then what Saul tried to do. They just go about it in different ways. Just entertain them and we have the masses. Many people go to church to be entertained. The Church gathers to worship.

John 4:24

God is a Spirit: and they that worship him must worship him in spirit and in truth.

Acts 6:8-15 **A history lesson taught by Stephen that got he killed.**

And Stephen, full of faith and power, did great wonders and miracles among the people. Then there arose certain of the synagogue, which is called the synagogue of the Libertines, and Cyrenians, and Alexandrians, and of them of Cilicia and of Asia, disputing with Stephen. And they were not able to resist the wisdom and the spirit by which he spake. Then they suborned men, which said, We have heard him speak blasphemous words against Moses, and against God. And they stirred up the people, and the elders, and the scribes, and came upon him, and caught him, and brought him to the council, And set up false witnesses, which said, This man ceaseth not to speak blasphemous words against this holy place, and the law: For we have heard him say, that this Jesus of Nazareth shall destroy this place, and shall change the customs which Moses delivered us. And all that sat in the council, looking stedfastly on him, saw his face as it had been the face of an angel.

Acts 7: 1- 58

Then said the high priest, Are these things so? And he said, Men, brethren, and fathers, hearken; The God of glory appeared unto our father Abraham, when he was in Mesopotamia, before he dwelt in Charran, And said unto him, Get thee out of thy country, and from thy kindred, and come into the land which I shall shew thee. Then came he out of the land of the Chaldaeans, and dwelt in Charran: and from thence, when his father was dead, he removed him into this land, wherein ye now dwell. And he gave him none inheritance in it, no, not so much as to set his foot on: yet he promised that he would give it to him for a possession, and to his seed after him, when as yet he had no child. And God spake on this wise, That his seed should sojourn in a strange land; and that they should bring them into bondage, and entreat them evil four hundred years. And the nation to whom they shall be in bondage will I judge, said God: and after that shall they come forth, and serve me in this place. And he gave him the covenant of circumcision: and so Abraham begat Isaac, and circumcised him the eighth day; and Isaac begat Jacob; and Jacob begat the twelve patriarchs. And the patriarchs, moved with envy, sold Joseph into Egypt: but God was with him, And delivered him out of all his afflictions, and gave him favour and wisdom in the sight of Pharaoh king of Egypt; and he made him governor over Egypt and all his house. Now there came a dearth over all the land of Egypt and Chanaan, and great affliction: and our fathers found no sustenance. But when Jacob heard that there was corn in Egypt, he sent out our fathers first. And at the second time Joseph was made known to his brethren; and Joseph's kindred was made known unto Pharaoh. Then sent Joseph, and called his father Jacob to him, and all his kindred, threescore and fifteen souls. So Jacob went down into Egypt, and died, he, and our fathers, And were carried over into Sychem, and laid in the sepulchre that Abraham bought for a sum of money of the sons of Emmor the father of Sychem. But when the time of the promise drew nigh, which God had sworn to Abraham, the people grew and multiplied in Egypt, Till another king arose, which knew not Joseph. The same dealt subtilly with our kindred, and evil entreated our fathers, so that they cast out their young children, to the end they might not live. In which time Moses was born, and was exceeding fair, and nourished up in his father's house three months: And when he was cast out, Pharaoh's daughter took him up, and nourished him for her own son. And Moses was learned in all the wisdom of the Egyptians, and was mighty in words and in deeds. And when he was full forty years old, it came into his heart to visit his brethren the children of Israel. And seeing one of them suffer wrong, he defended him, and avenged him that was oppressed, and smote the Egyptian: For he supposed his brethren would have understood how that God by his hand would deliver them: but they understood not. And the next day he shewed himself unto them as they strove, and would have set them at one again, saying, Sirs, ye are brethren; why do ye wrong one to another? But he that did his neighbour wrong thrust him away, saying, Who made thee a ruler and a judge over us? Wilt thou kill me, as thou diddest the Egyptian yesterday? Then fled Moses at this saying, and was a stranger in the land of Madian, where he begat two sons. And when forty years were expired, there appeared to him in the wilderness of mount Sina an angel of the Lord in a flame of fire in a bush. When Moses saw it, he wondered at the sight: and as he drew near to behold it, the voice of the LORD came unto him, Saying, I am the God of thy fathers, the God of Abraham, and the God of Isaac, and the God of Jacob. Then Moses trembled, and durst not behold. Then said the Lord to him, Put off thy shoes from thy feet: for the place where thou standest is holy ground. I have seen, I have seen the affliction of my people which is in Egypt, and I have heard their groaning, and am come down to deliver them. And now come, I will send thee into Egypt. This Moses whom they refused, saying, Who made thee a ruler and a judge? the same did God send to be a ruler and a deliverer by the hand of the angel which appeared to him in the bush. He brought them out, after that he had shewed wonders and signs in the land of Egypt, and in the Red sea, and in the wilderness forty years. This is that Moses, which said unto the children of Israel, A prophet shall the Lord your God raise up unto you of your brethren, like unto me; him shall ye hear. This is he, that was in the church in the wilderness with the angel which spake to him in the mount Sina, and with our fathers: who received the lively oracles to give unto us: To whom our fathers would not obey, but thrust him from them, and in their hearts turned back again into Egypt, Saying unto Aaron, Make us gods to go before us: for as for this Moses, which brought us out of the land of Egypt, we wot not what is become of him. And they made a calf in those days, and offered sacrifice unto the idol, and rejoiced in the works of their own hands. Then God turned, and gave them up to worship the host of heaven; as it is written in the book of the prophets, O ye house of Israel, have ye offered to me slain beasts and sacrifices by the space of forty years in the wilderness? Yea, ye took up the tabernacle of

Moloch, and the star of your god Remphan, figures which ye made to worship them: and I will carry you away beyond Babylon. Our fathers had the tabernacle of witness in the wilderness, as he had appointed, speaking unto Moses, that he should make it according to the fashion that he had seen. Which also our fathers that came after brought in with Jesus into the possession of the Gentiles, whom God drave out before the face of our fathers, unto the days of David; Who found favour before God, and desired to find a tabernacle for the God of Jacob. But Solomon built him an house. Howbeit the most High dwelleth not in temples made with hands; as saith the prophet, Heaven is my throne, and earth is my footstool: what house will ye build me? saith the Lord: or what is the place of my rest? Hath not my hand made all these things? Ye stiffnecked and uncircumcised in heart and ears, ye do always resist the Holy Ghost: as your fathers did, so do ye. Which of the prophets have not your fathers persecuted? and they have slain them which shewed before of the coming of the Just One; of whom ye have been now the betrayers and murderers: Who have received the law by the disposition of angels, and have not kept it. When they heard these things, they were cut to the heart, and they gnashed on him with their teeth. But he, being full of the Holy Ghost, looked up stedfastly into heaven, and saw the glory of God, and Jesus standing on the right hand of God, And said, Behold, I see the heavens opened, and the Son of man standing on the right hand of God. Then they cried out with a loud voice, and stopped their ears, and ran upon him with one accord, And cast him out of the city, and stoned him: **and the witnesses laid down their clothes at a young man's feet, whose name was Saul.**

*When I give you a verse, please take the time and read the whole chapter around that verse in your Bible, so you can get the complete understanding of that verse. I am trying to help you study your Bible for yourself. What you read in the Bible you will not forget. I believe the Holy Spirit will see to that. From the verses you have just read, is the first time this Saul come into the picture in God's word.

Acts 8:1- 4 Saul's approval of Stephen death.

And Saul was consenting unto his death. And at that time there was a great persecution against the church which was at Jerusalem; and they were all scattered abroad throughout the regions of Judaea and Samaria, except the apostles. And devout men carried Stephen to his burial, and made great lamentation over him. As for Saul, he made havock of the church, entering into every house, and haling men and women committed them to prison. Therefore they that were scattered abroad went every where preaching the word.

*Havock / Havoc – wide destruction; great confusion.

Acts 9:1-2

 And Saul, yet breathing out threatenings and slaughter against the disciples of the Lord, went unto the high priest, And desired of him letters to Damascus to the synagogues, that if he found any of this way, whether they were men or women, he might bring them bound unto Jerusalem.

*Saul failed to stop the Lord's Church then, and the Church has endured until this day. The Gospel of Jesus has never stopped being taught. Many of you may not know these French words: Griot, Jali, and Jeli. These are names called of African storytellers. These storytellers handed information down thru their tribes of past events in their history. Because in many cases nothing was written down. The "Jews-Israelites" practiced the same thing in their tribes as well. The Gospel of Jesus was taught the same way until we received the Bible as we have it now. Even though we have the Bible, we have to take the Bible and teach the Gospel to other.

Listen to something Jesus said while on earth.

John 6:45

It is written in the prophets, And they shall be all taught of God. Every man therefore that hath heard, and hath learned of the Father, cometh unto me.

*I ask the question, have you ever been taught the gospel? Do you really know what the Gospel is. Saul did not know the Gospel and how applies to his life.

* Saul's Conversion to Christianity.

I want you take notice of what Saul said about baptism and after he was converted why was he was baptized.

Romans 6:3-4

Know ye not, that so many of us as were baptized into Jesus Christ were baptized into his death? Therefore we are buried with him by baptism into death: that like as Christ was raised up from the dead by the glory of the Father, even so we also should walk in newness of life.

Acts 2:38

Then Peter said unto them, Repent, and be baptized every one of you in the name of Jesus Christ for the remission of sins, and ye shall receive the gift of the Holy Ghost

*We are forgiven of sin thru baptism. Why was Saul Baptized, for the same reason.

Acts 9:1-24 Saul became a Christian.

And Saul, yet breathing out threatenings and slaughter against the disciples of the Lord, went unto the high priest, And desired of him letters to Damascus to the synagogues, that if he found any of this way, whether they were men or women, he might bring them bound unto Jerusalem. And as he journeyed, he came near Damascus: and suddenly there shined round about him a light from heaven: And he fell to the earth, and heard a voice saying unto him, Saul, Saul, why persecutest thou me? And he said, Who art thou, Lord? And the Lord said, I am Jesus whom thou persecutest: it is hard for thee to kick against the pricks. And he trembling and astonished said, Lord, what wilt thou have me to do? And the Lord said unto him, Arise, and go into the city, and it shall be told thee what thou must do. And the men which journeyed with him stood speechless, hearing a voice, but seeing no man. And Saul arose from the earth; and when his eyes were opened, he saw no man: but they led him by the hand, and brought him into Damascus. And he was three days without sight, and neither did eat nor drink. And there was a certain disciple at Damascus, named Ananias; and to him said the Lord in a vision, Ananias. And he said, Behold, I am here, Lord. And the Lord said unto him, Arise, and go into the street which is called Straight, and enquire in the house of Judas for one called Saul, of Tarsus: for, behold, he prayeth. And hath seen in a vision a man named Ananias coming in, and putting his hand on him, that he might receive his sight. Then Ananias answered, Lord, I have heard by many of this man, how much evil he hath done to thy saints at Jerusalem: And here he hath authority from the chief priests to bind all that call on thy name. But the Lord said unto him, Go thy way: for he is a chosen vessel unto me, to bear my name before the Gentiles, and kings, and the children of Israel: For I will shew him how great things he must suffer for my name's sake. And Ananias went his way, and entered into the house; and putting his hands on him said, Brother Saul, the Lord, even Jesus, that appeared unto thee in the way as thou camest, hath sent me, that thou mightest receive thy sight, and be filled with the Holy Ghost. And immediately there fell from his eyes as it had been scales: and he received sight forthwith, and arose, **and was baptized.** And when he had received meat, he was strengthened. Then was Saul certain days with the disciples which were at Damascus. And straightway he preached Christ in the synagogues, that he is the Son of God. But all that heard him were amazed, and said; Is not this he that destroyed them which called on this name in Jerusalem, and came hither for that intent, that he might bring them bound unto the chief priests? But Saul increased the more in strength, and confounded the Jews which dwelt at Damascus, proving that this is very Christ. And after that many days were fulfilled, the Jews took counsel to kill him: But their laying await was known of Saul. And they watched the gates day and night to kill him.

*Many are just like Saul when they hear truth they harden their minds to it. Jesus Church is still here on earth. You just have to be honest with yourself to find it. Saul accepted Christianity, but he fought it hard at first.

Chapter 3

JESUS

Do you think God, Jesus and the Holy Spirit are one and the same? Let us take a good look and see who Jesus is.

1John 5:4-13

*Jesus is God's Son, and they are one in the record they bare. In one accord in word, thought and deed.

For whatsoever is born of God overcometh the world: and this is the victory that overcometh the world, even our faith. Who is he that overcometh the world, but he that believeth that Jesus is the Son of God? This is he that came by water and blood, even Jesus Christ; not by water only, but by water and blood. And it is the Spirit that beareth witness, because the Spirit is truth. For there are three that bear record in heaven, the Father, the Word, and the Holy Ghost: and these three are one. And there are three that bear witness in earth, the Spirit, and the water, and the blood: and these three agree in one. If we receive the witness of men, the witness of God is greater: for this is the witness of God which he hath testified of his Son. He that believeth on the Son of God hath the witness in himself: he that believeth not God hath made him a liar; because he believeth not the record that God gave of his Son. And this is the record, that God hath given to us eternal life, and this life is in his Son. He that hath the Son hath life; and he that hath not the Son of God hath not life. These things have I written unto you that believe on the name of the Son of God; that ye may know that ye have eternal life, and that ye may believe on the name of the Son of God.

Genesis 1:1

In the beginning God created the heaven and the earth.

*Scientific investigators has come up with several composites that make up the world. In the beginning – time, God – force, created – energy, heavens – space, and the earth – matter. I can accept their findings. But some fail to accept there is a God. The way they put it, intelligent design. If this be the case, the earth could have come into existence by aliens. Take notice of something Jesus said while hanging on the cross before he died.

John 17:1-5

These words spake Jesus, and lifted up his eyes to heaven, and said, Father, the hour is come; glorify thy Son, that thy Son also may glorify thee: As thou hast given him power over all flesh, that he should give eternal life to as many as thou hast given him. And this is life eternal, that they might know thee the only true God, and Jesus Christ, whom thou hast sent. I have glorified thee on the earth: I have finished the work which thou gavest me to do. And now, O Father, glorify thou me with thine own self with the glory which I had with thee **before the world was.**

*Jesus said He was with God before it was a world.

Genesis 1:26-27

And God said, Let us make man in our image, after our likeness: and let them have dominion over the fish of the sea, and over the fowl of the air, and over the cattle, and over all the earth, and over every creeping thing that creepeth upon the earth. So God created man in his own image, in the image of God created he him; male and female created he them.

*Let us make man. God, Jesus-the word and the Holy Spirit.

Philippians 2:5-11

Let this mind be in you, which was also in Christ Jesus: Who, being in the form of God, thought it not robbery to be **equal with God:** But made himself of no reputation, and took upon him the form of a servant, and was made in the likeness of men: And being found in fashion as a man, he humbled himself, and became obedient unto death, even the death of the cross. Wherefore God also hath highly exalted him, and given him a name which is above every name: That at the name of Jesus every knee should bow, of things in heaven, and things in earth, and things under the earth; And that every tongue should confess that Jesus Christ is Lord, to the glory of God the Father.

*Equal with God.

John 14:1-17

Let not your heart be troubled: ye believe in God, believe also in me. In my Father's house are many mansions: if it were not so, I would have told you. I go to prepare a place for you. And if I go and prepare a place for you, I will come again, and receive you unto myself; that where I am, there ye may be also. And whither I go ye know, and the way ye know. Thomas saith unto him, Lord, we know not whither thou goest; and how can we know the way? Jesus saith unto him, I am the way, the truth, and the life: no man cometh unto the Father, but by me. If ye had known me, ye should have known my Father also: and from henceforth ye know him, and have seen him. Philip saith unto him, Lord, show us the Father, and it sufficeth us. Jesus saith unto him, Have I been so long time with you, and yet hast thou not known me, Philip? he that hath seen me hath seen the Father; and how sayest thou then, Show us the Father? Believest thou not that I am in the Father, and the Father in me? the words that I speak unto you I speak not of myself: but the Father that dwelleth in me, he doeth the works. Believe me that I am in the Father, and the Father in me: or else believe me for the very works' sake. Verily, verily, I say unto you, He that believeth on me, the works that I do shall he do also; and greater works than these shall he do; because I go unto my Father. And whatsoever ye shall ask in my name, that will I do, that the Father may be glorified in the Son. If ye shall ask any thing in my name, I will do it. If ye love me, keep my commandments. And I will pray the Father, and he shall give you another Comforter, that he may abide with you for ever; Even the Spirit of truth; whom the world cannot receive, because it seeth him not, neither knoweth him: but ye know him; for he dwelleth with you, and shall be in you.

*Jesus was speaking of three distinctive masculine personalities. The Father-God, Himself and the Holy Spirit.

Chapter 4

PATRIARCHAL AGE

Some think the Bible cannot be understood and even contradicts itself. In order to understand the Bible there are some things you need to know. First there is the Old Testament and the New Testament. The Old Testament does not govern our lives today. After Jesus rose from the dead, we live under the New Testament.

*Hebrews 9:15 - Jesus died for the New Testament

And for this cause he is the mediator of the New Testament that by means of death, for the redemption of the transgressions that were under the first testament, they which are called might receive the promise of eternal inheritance.

*There are three periods of Bible History we need to understand to truly understand God's word. They are the Patriarchal, Mosaic and Christian Age. If you do know of these times in history, the Bible can seems to contradict itself. I am going give you a brief high-light of each of these ages. When you study your Bible and you want to study salvation and Jesus Church, the key is to stay focused on the Promise and on Jesus. Start watching what God promises Abram in Genesis 12:1-3 and follow the Promise from here down thru the New Testament. This Promise is our Lord and Saviour Jesus Christ. Those of the Promise is saved in Jesus Church. Also take notice that most scriptures of distinction have an companion verse.

*Example of a companion verse:

Genesis 3:15 Satan will bruise Jesus heel.

And I will put enmity between thee and the woman, and between thy seed and her seed; it shall bruise thy head, and thou shalt bruise his heel.

John 13:18 Judas Iscariot lifted up his heel against Jesus.

I speak not of you all: I know whom I have chosen: but that the scripture may be fulfilled, He that eateth bread with me hath lifted up his heel against me.

*From our studies of God's word, we know that Satan used the serpent as a tool to make Adam and Eve to sin. Satan bruised Jesus heel through His death on the cross. But Jesus bruised Satan's head thru raising from the dead.

Matthew 5:17 Jesus fulfil what was said in Genesis 3:15.

Think not that I am come to destroy the law, or the prophets: I am not come to destroy, but to fulfil.

The Patriarchal Age

The Bible begins and ends with God.

Genesis 1:1

In the beginning God created the heaven and the earth.

Revelation 22:13

I am Alpha and Omega, the beginning and the end, the first and the last.

Patriarch

A Patriarch is the father of a tribe. The name given to the head of a family or tribe in the Old Testament. In the beginning of Bible History there was no written documents for mankind to read. God expressed his commands to the family head and he told the others what God expected of them. Abraham and David were two of these patriarch.

Acts 2:29 David

Men and brethren, let me freely speak unto you of the patriarch David, that he is both dead and buried, and his sepulchre is with us unto this day.

Hebrews 7:4 Abraham

Now consider how great this man was, unto whom even the patriarch Abraham gave the tenth of the spoils.

*In the beginning of Bible History if you would notice God had a personal relationship with Adam. Before Adam sin took place in The Garden of Eden.

Genesis 2:1-25

Verses: 7-9

And the LORD God formed man of the dust of the ground, and breathed into his nostrils the breath of life; and man became a living soul. And the LORD God planted a garden eastward in Eden; and there he put the man whom he had formed. And out of the ground made the LORD God to grow every tree that is pleasant to the sight, and good for food; the tree of life also in the midst of the garden, and the tree of knowledge of good and evil.

Verses: 15-25

And the LORD God took the man, and put him into the garden of Eden to dress it and to keep it. And the LORD God commanded the man, saying, Of every tree of the garden thou mayest freely eat: But of the tree of the knowledge of good and evil, thou shalt not eat of it: for in the day that thou eatest thereof thou shalt surely die. And the LORD God said, It is not good that the man should be alone; I will make him an help meet for him. And out of the ground the LORD God formed every beast of the field, and every fowl of the air; and brought them unto Adam to see what he would call them: and whatsoever Adam called every living creature, that was the name thereof. And Adam gave names to all cattle, and to the fowl of the air, and to every beast of the field; but for Adam there was not found an help meet for him. And the LORD God caused a deep sleep to fall upon Adam, and he slept: and he took one of his ribs, and closed up the flesh instead thereof; And the rib, which the LORD God had taken from man, made he a woman, and brought her unto the man. And Adam said, This is now bone of my bones, and flesh of my flesh: she shall be called Woman, because she was taken out of Man. Therefore shall a man leave his father and his mother, and shall cleave unto his wife: and they shall be one flesh. And they were both naked, the man and his wife, and were not ashamed.

*Food for thought verse V- 24: And Adam said, this is now bone of my bones, and flesh of my flesh: she shall be called Woman, because she was taken out of Man. Therefore shall a man leave his father and his mother, and shall cleave unto his wife: and they shall be one flesh. **(Marriage is between a man and a woman).**

Genesis 3:1-24 The sin that ended mankind personal contact with God.

Now the serpent was more subtil than any beast of the field which the LORD God had made. And he said unto the woman, Yea, hath God said, Ye shall not eat of every tree of the garden? And the woman said unto the serpent, We may eat of the fruit of the trees of the garden: But of the fruit of the tree which is in the midst of the garden, God hath said, **Ye shall not eat of it, neither shall ye touch it, lest ye die. And the serpent said unto the woman, Ye shall not surely die:** For God doth know that in the day ye eat thereof, then your eyes shall be opened, and ye shall be as gods, knowing good and evil. And when the woman saw that the tree was good for food, and that it was pleasant to the eyes, and a tree to be desired to make one wise, she took of the fruit thereof, and did eat, and gave also unto her husband with her; and he did eat. And the eyes of them both were opened, and they knew that they were naked; and they sewed fig leaves together, and made themselves aprons. And they heard the voice of the LORD God walking in the garden in the cool of the day: and Adam and his wife hid themselves from the presence of the LORD God amongst the trees of the garden. And the LORD God called unto Adam, and said unto him, Where art thou? And he said, I heard thy voice in the garden, and I was afraid, because I was naked; and I hid myself. And he said, Who told thee that thou wast naked? Hast thou eaten of the tree, whereof I commanded thee that thou shouldest not eat? And the man said, The woman whom thou gavest to be with me, she gave me of the tree, and I did eat. And the LORD God said unto the woman, What is this that thou hast done? And the woman said, The serpent beguiled me, and I did eat. And the LORD God said unto the serpent, Because thou hast done this, thou art cursed above all cattle, and above every beast of the field; upon thy belly shalt thou go, and dust shalt thou eat all the days of thy life: And I will put enmity between thee and the woman, and between thy seed and her seed; it shall bruise thy head, and thou shalt bruise his heel. Unto the woman he said, I will greatly multiply thy sorrow and thy conception; in sorrow thou shalt bring forth children; and thy desire shall be to thy husband, and he shall rule over thee. And unto Adam he said, Because thou hast hearkened unto the voice of thy wife, and hast eaten of the tree, of which I commanded thee, saying, Thou shalt not eat of it: cursed is the ground for thy sake; in sorrow shalt thou eat of it all the days of thy life; Thorns also and thistles shall it bring forth to thee; and thou shalt eat the herb of the field; In the sweat of thy face shalt thou eat bread, till thou return unto the ground; for out of it wast thou taken: for dust thou art, and unto dust shalt thou return. And Adam called his wife's name Eve; because she was the mother of all living. Unto Adam also and to his wife did the LORD God make coats of skins, and clothed them. And the LORD God said, Behold, the man is become as one of us, to know good and evil: and now, lest he put forth his hand, and take also of the tree of life, and eat, and live for ever: Therefore the LORD God sent him forth from the garden of Eden, to till the ground from whence he was taken. So he drove out the man; and he placed at the east of the garden of Eden Cherubims, and a flaming sword which turned every way, to keep the way of the tree of life.

*Surely die. Adam and Eve thought they would physically die but when they ate of the tree of knowledge of good and evil they died spiritually. That is why the serpent said you will not surely die. Sin is a violation against the laws of God. They started dying physically when they were put out of the Garden of Eden away from the tree of life. That day mankind lost his personal association with God. God knew man would sin, and He also knew the cleverness of the serpent because He made him. Genesis 2:16-17, God commanded man not to eat of the tree of knowledge of good and evil, but He made man a being that could make choices.

John 4:24

God is a Spirit: and they that worship him must worship him in spirit and in truth.

*What John says here is not a statement of choice. But many fail to do this today. But it is their choice. God sent Jesus into the world to get back that fellowship with mankind that was lost in the garden.

Romans 5:14-17

Nevertheless death reigned from Adam to Moses, even over them that had not sinned after the similitude of Adam's transgression, who is the figure of him that was to come. But not as the offence, so also is the free gift. For if through the offence of one many be dead, much more the grace of God, and the gift by grace, which is by one man, Jesus Christ, hath abounded unto many. And not as it was by one that sinned, so is the gift: for the judgment was by one to condemnation, but the free gift is of many offences unto justification. For if by one man's offence death reigned by one; much more they which receive abundance of grace and of the gift of righteousness shall reign in life by one, Jesus Christ.)

1Corinthians 15:22

For as in Adam all die, even so in Christ shall all be made alive.

Genesis 12:1-3 The Promise God gave to mankind – Jesus.

Now the LORD had said unto Abram, Get thee out of thy country, and from thy kindred, and from thy father's house, unto a land that I will shew thee: And I will make of thee a great nation, and I will bless thee, and make thy name great; and thou shalt be a blessing: And I will bless them that bless thee, and curse him that curseth thee: and in thee shall all families of the earth be blessed.

*The Bible addresses two classes of people, Jews and Gentiles. These are the families of the earth to be blessed. The next period of Bible History is The Mosaic Age. But before we go from here, I want to say something about it. The Mosaic Age is a very domineering age. If you are not careful it could make you overlook the Patriarchal Age. To fail to understand the Patriarchal Age, you will miss out on Jesus purpose on earth and His Church. The Patriarchal Age set the stage to Jesus. The Patriarchal Age began at the creation and ends at the Mosaic Age. In my conclusion of the

Patriarchal Age, I want you to take notice of something Paul said to the Galatians.

Galatians 3:8 Paul

And the scripture, foreseeing that God would justify the heathen through faith, preached before the gospel unto Abraham, saying, In thee shall all nations be blessed.

*The heathen here is in reference to the Gentiles. The Gospel is for all mankind, Jews and Gentiles alike.

Matthew 28:18-20 Jesus

Go ye therefore, and teach all nations, baptizing them in the name of the Father, and of the Son, and of the Holy Ghost: Teaching them to observe all things whatsoever I have commanded you: and, lo, I am with you always, even unto the end of the world. Amen.

*Jesus is instructing the Apostles to teach the Gospel to all nations.

Mark 16:15-16 Jesus

And he said unto them, Go ye into all the world, and preach the gospel to every creature. He that believeth and is baptized shall be saved; but he that believeth not shall be damned.

*When someone is taught the Gospel and they accept it and is baptized, the Lord adds you to His Church - Acts 2:47.

1Corinthians 15:1- 4 Paul's definition of the Gospel.

Moreover, brethren, I declare unto you the gospel which I preached unto you, which also ye have received, and wherein ye stand; By which also ye are saved, if ye keep in memory what I preached unto you, unless ye have believed in vain. For I delivered unto you first of all that which I also received, how that **Christ died for our sins according to the scriptures; And that he was buried, and that he rose again the third day according to the scriptures:**

*When we get to the Christian Age. You will see how all this comes together and how we must be sure we are in Jesus Church. Can you identify your church with all been said thus for?

Chapter 5

THE MOSAIC AGE

Named after Moses thru whom God gave the Ten Commandments to the Jews. Jacob's twelve sons make up the tribes of Israel / Jews in which is one and the same people. Moses was born under the Patriarch Age. Listen to what Moses told these people concerning God will for them.

Deuteronomy 5:1-7

And Moses called all Israel, and said unto them, Hear, O Israel, the statutes and judgments which I speak in your ears this day, that ye may learn them, and keep, and do them. The LORD our God made a covenant with us in Horeb. **The LORD made not this covenant with our fathers, but with us, even us, who are all of us here alive this day.** The LORD talked with you face to face in the mount out of the midst of the fire, (I stood between the LORD and you at that time, to shew you the word of the LORD: for ye were afraid by reason of the fire, and went not up into the mount;) saying, I am the LORD thy God, which brought thee out of the land of Egypt, from the house of bondage. Thou shalt have none other gods before me.

*If you would read further in your Bible in chapter five you will see God through Moses went on to show Israel how to treat each other. Moses makes no mention of Gentiles.

*Jesus was born under the Law of Moses or The Ten Commandment Law. Jesus was the only one to live under this law without sin.

1Peter 2:22 Jesus

Who did no sin, neither was guile found in his mouth:

2Corinthians 5:21 Jesus

For he hath made him to be sin for us, who knew no sin; that we might be made the righteousness of God in him.

*Under the Law of Moses, there were many things they had to do. Animal sacrifice is one that many today could not do. But do not consider this when they try to add the Law of Moses with the law of Christ. Take notice to what James said of the Law of Moses.

James 2:10

For whosoever shall keep the whole law, and yet offend in one point, he is guilty of all.

Hebrews 10:28 Paul

He that despised Moses' law died without mercy under two or three witnesses:

*I have not seen any church organization killing anyone for sinning. Have you seen this happen lately?

*Many people today try to incorporate the Law of Moses into the Law of Christ. This is not new, in the Apostles day they were doing this as well. Let us take a look at one of these cases. Under the influence of Judaizing teachers, sought to incorporate Law of Moses with Christianity.

Galatians 3:1-29

Galatians 3:1-8

O foolish Galatians, who hath bewitched you, that ye should not obey the truth, before whose eyes Jesus Christ hath been evidently set forth, crucified among you? This only would I learn of you, Received ye the Spirit by the works of the law, or by the hearing of faith? Are ye so foolish? having begun in the Spirit, are ye now made perfect by the flesh? Have ye suffered so many things in vain? if it be yet in vain. He therefore that ministereth to you the Spirit, and worketh miracles among you, doeth he it by the works of the law, or by the hearing of faith? Even as Abraham believed God, and it was accounted to him for righteousness. **Know ye therefore that they which are of faith, the same are the children of Abraham. And the scripture, foreseeing that God would justify the heathen through faith, preached before the gospel unto Abraham, saying, In thee shall all nations be blessed.**

*Justify the Heathen / Gentiles through faith. Here Paul is rehearsing to them Genesis 12:1-3/ Patriarch Age.

Verse 3 And I will bless them that bless thee, and curse him that curseth thee: and in thee shall all families of the earth be blessed.

Galatians 3:9-14

So then they which be of faith are blessed with faithful Abraham. For as many as are of the works of the law are under the curse: for it is written, Cursed is every one that continueth not in all things which are written in the book of the law to do them. **But that no man is justified by the law in the sight of God**, it is evident: for, The just shall live by faith. And the law is not of faith: but, The man that doeth them shall live in them. **Christ hath redeemed us from the curse of the law**, being made a curse for us: for it is written, Cursed is every one that hangeth on a tree: **That the blessing of Abraham might come on the Gentiles through Jesus Christ**; that we might receive the promise of the Spirit through faith.

*Christ came into world to save all mankind, not just the Jews.

Galatians 3:16-19 Promise - Jesus

Now to Abraham and his seed were the promises made. He saith not, And to seeds, as of many; but as of one, And to thy seed, which is Christ. And this I say, that the covenant, that was confirmed before of God in Christ, the law, which was four hundred and thirty years after, cannot disannul, that it should make the promise of none effect. **For if the inheritance be of the law, it is no more of promise:** but God gave it to Abraham by promise. **Wherefore then serveth the law? It was added because of transgressions,** till the seed should come to whom the promise was made; and it was ordained by angels in the hand of a mediator.

*The Law was added because of sin. Also the Law of Moses was given to the Jews four hundred and thirty years after God made his promise to Abraham.

Galatians 3:24-29 The Law of Moses was our schoolmaster.

Wherefore the law was our schoolmaster to bring us unto Christ, that we might be justified by faith. But after that faith is come, we are no longer under a schoolmaster. For ye are all the children of God by faith in Christ Jesus. **For as many of you as have been baptized into Christ have put on Christ.** There is neither Jew nor Greek, there is neither bond nor free, there is neither male nor female: **for ye are all one in Christ Jesus.** And if ye be Christ's, then are ye Abraham's seed, and heirs according to the promise.

(Baptism puts Jew and Gentile in Christ Jesus).

*We are all one in Christ Jesus / Jew and Gentile. This was not the case under the Law of Moses. The Law of Moses was only for Israel-Jews.

*Food for thought: I have tried my best to keep my opinion out of these writing, because I want you see God word for yourself. This book is a tool for learning.

Ephesians 2:11-22 Gentiles aliens from the Israel.

Wherefore remember, that ye being in time past Gentiles in the flesh, who are called Uncircumcision by that which is called the Circumcision in the flesh made by hands; **That at that time ye were without Christ, being aliens from the commonwealth of Israel, and strangers from the covenants of promise, having no hope, and without God in the world:** But now in Christ Jesus ye who sometimes were far off are made nigh by the blood of Christ. For he is our peace, **who hath made both one**, and hath broken down the middle wall of partition between us; Having abolished in his flesh the enmity, even the law of commandments contained in ordinances; for to make in himself of twain one new man, so making peace; And that he might **reconcile both unto God in one body by the cross, having slain the enmity thereby: And came and preached peace to you which were afar off, and to them that were nigh.** For through him we both have access by one Spirit unto the Father. **Now therefore ye are no more strangers and foreigners, but fellowcitizens with the saints, and of the household of God;** And are built upon the foundation of the apostles and prophets, Jesus Christ himself being the chief corner stone; In whom all the building fitly framed together groweth unto an holy temple in the Lord: In whom ye also are builded together for an habitation of God through the Spirit.

Chapter 6

THE CHRISTIAN AGE

Genesis 12: 1-3

Now the LORD had said unto Abram, Get thee out of thy country, and from thy kindred, and from thy father's house, unto a land that I will shew thee: And I will make of thee a great nation, and I will bless thee, and make thy name great; and thou shalt be a blessing: And I will bless them that bless thee, and curse him that curseth thee: and in thee shall **all families of the earth be blessed.**

*Jesus is the fulfillment of this prophecy.

Hebrews 9:11-15 Jesus

But Christ being come an high priest of good things to come, by a greater and more perfect tabernacle, not made with hands, that is to say, not of this building; Neither by the blood of goats and calves, but by his own blood he entered in once into the holy place, having obtained eternal redemption for us. For if the blood of bulls and of goats, and the ashes of an heifer sprinkling the unclean, sanctifieth to the purifying of the flesh: How much more shall the blood of Christ, who through the eternal Spirit offered himself without spot to God, purge your conscience from dead works to serve the living God? **And for this cause he is the mediator of the new testament,** that by means of death, for the redemption of the transgressions that were **under the first testament**, they which are called might **receive the promise of eternal inheritance.**

*Jesus is the promise of eternal inheritance that was promised to Abraham. All families of the earth will be blessed - Genesis 12.

Matthew 1:18-23 Jesus

 Now the birth of Jesus Christ was on this wise: When as his mother Mary was espoused to Joseph, before they came together, she was found with child of the Holy Ghost.Then Joseph her husband, being a just man, and not willing to make her a public example, was minded to put her away privily. But while he thought on these things, behold, the angel of the LORD appeared unto him in a dream, saying, Joseph, thou son of David, fear not to take unto thee Mary thy wife: for that which is conceived in her is of the Holy Ghost. **And she shall bring forth a son, and thou shalt call his name JESUS: for he shall save his people from their sins.** Now all this was done, that it might be fulfilled which was spoken of the Lord by the prophet, saying, Behold, a virgin shall be with child, and shall bring forth a son, and they shall call his name Emmanuel, which being interpreted is, God with us.

Luke 2:25-40 Jesus

 And when the days of her purification according to the law of Moses were accomplished, they brought him to Jerusalem, to present him to the Lord; (As it is written in the law of the LORD, Every male that openeth the womb shall be called holy to the Lord;) And to offer a sacrifice according to that which is said in the law of the Lord, A pair of turtledoves, or two young pigeons. And, behold, there was a man in Jerusalem, whose name was Simeon; and the same man was just and devout, waiting for the consolation of Israel: and the Holy Ghost was upon him. And it was revealed unto him by the Holy Ghost, that he should not see death, before he had seen the Lord's Christ.

And he came by the Spirit into the temple: and when the parents brought in the child Jesus, to do for him after the custom of the law, Then took he him up in his arms, and blessed God, and said, Lord, now lettest thou thy servant depart in peace, according to thy word: For mine eyes have seen thy salvation, Which thou hast prepared before the face of all people; A light to lighten the Gentiles, and the glory of thy people Israel. And Joseph and his mother marvelled at those things which were spoken of him. And Simeon blessed them, and said unto Mary his mother, Behold, this child is set for the fall and rising again of many in Israel; and for a sign which shall be spoken against; (Yea, a sword shall pierce through thy own soul also,) that the thoughts of many hearts may be revealed. And there was one Anna, a prophetess, the daughter of Phanuel, of the tribe of Aser: she was of a great age, and had lived with an husband seven years from her virginity; And she was a widow of about fourscore and four years, which departed not from the temple, but served God with fastings and prayers night and day. And she coming in that instant gave thanks likewise unto the Lord, and spake of him to all them that looked for redemption in Jerusalem. And when they had performed all things according to the law of the Lord, they returned into Galilee, to their own city Nazareth. And the child grew, and waxed strong in spirit, filled with wisdom: and the grace of God was upon him.

*The Christian Age carries the name of Jesus. Because He is the promised one that was to come into world and reconcile all mankind back to God.

John 17:1- 26 Jesus's prayer for His Disciples

These words spake Jesus, and lifted up his eyes to heaven, and said, Father, the hour is come; glorify thy Son, that thy Son also may glorify thee: As thou hast given him power over all flesh, that he should give eternal life to as many as thou hast given him.

And this is life eternal, that they might know thee the only true God, and Jesus Christ, whom thou hast sent. I have glorified thee on the earth: **I have finished the work which thou gavest me to do.** And now, O Father, glorify thou me with thine own self with the glory which I had with thee before the world was. **I have manifested thy name unto the men which thou gavest me out of the world:** thine they were, and thou gavest them me; and they have kept thy word. Now they have known that all things whatsoever thou hast given me are of thee. For I have given unto them the words which thou gavest me; and they have received them, and have known surely that I came out from thee, and they have believed that thou didst send me. I pray for them: I pray not for the world, but for them which thou hast given me; for they are thine. And all mine are thine, and thine are mine; and I am glorified in them. And now I am no more in the world, but these are in the world, and I come to thee. Holy Father, keep through thine own name those whom thou hast given me, that they may be one, as we are. While I was with them in the world, I kept them in thy name: those that thou gavest me I have kept, and none of them is lost, **but the son of perdition;** that the scripture might be fulfilled. And now come I to thee; and these things I speak in the world, that they might have my joy fulfilled in themselves. **I have given them thy word;** and the world hath hated them, because they are not of the world, even as I am not of the world. I pray not that thou shouldest take them out of the world, but that thou shouldest keep them from the evil. They are not of the world, even as I am not of the world. **Sanctify them through thy truth: thy word is truth. As thou hast sent me into the world, even so have I also sent them into the world.** And for their sakes I sanctify myself, that they also might be sanctified through the truth. **Neither pray I for these alone, but for them also which shall believe on me through their word;** That they all may be one; as thou, Father, art in me, and I in thee, that they also may be one in us: that the world may believe that thou hast sent me. And the glory which thou gavest me I have given them; that they may be one, even as we are one: I in them, and thou in me, that they may be made perfect in one; and that the world may know that thou hast sent me, and hast loved them, as thou hast loved me. Father, I will that they also, whom thou hast given me, be with me where I am; that they may behold my glory, which thou hast given me: for thou lovedst me before the foundation of the world. O righteous Father, the world hath not known thee: but I have known thee, and these have known that thou hast sent me. And I have declared unto them thy name, and will declare it: that the love wherewith thou hast loved me may be in them, and I in them.

John 19:30 Jesus last words as He hung on the cross.

When Jesus therefore had received the vinegar, he said, **It is finished:** and he bowed his head, and gave up the ghost.

Mark 9:1-7 Jesus Kingdom -The Spiritual Church

And he said unto them, Verily I say unto you, That there be some of them that stand here, **which shall not taste of death**, till they have seen the **kingdom of God come with power.** And after six days Jesus taketh with him Peter, and James, and John, and leadeth them up into an high mountain apart by themselves: and he was transfigured before them. And his raiment became shining, exceeding white as snow; so as no fuller on earth can white them. And there appeared unto them Elias with Moses: and they were talking with Jesus. And Peter answered and said to Jesus, Master, it is good for us to be here: **and let us make three tabernacles; one for thee, and one for Moses, and one for Elias.** For he wist not what to say; for they were sore afraid. And there was a cloud that overshadowed them: and a voice came out of the cloud, saying, **This is my beloved Son: hear him.**

*Peter wanted to make three tabernacles, three churches. But a voice out of the cloud said hear my son. There are many churches in the world today teaching all kinds of doctrine of men. Jesus said He was going to build a Church. One Church, and we have to be sure we are in that Church. Now let us take notice when that Church came into existence and how to become a part of it. **We need also to take notice of Jesus commands to His Apostles.**

Acts 1:1-8

The former treatise have I made, O Theophilus, of all that Jesus began both to do and teach, Until the day in which he was taken up, after that he through the Holy Ghost had given commandments unto the apostles whom he had chosen: To whom also he shewed himself alive after his passion by many infallible proofs, being seen of them forty days, and speaking of the things pertaining to the kingdom of God: And, being assembled together with them, **commanded them that they should not depart from Jerusalem**, but **wait for the promise of the Father**, which, saith he, ye have heard of me. For John truly baptized with water; but ye shall be **baptized with the Holy Ghost** not many days hence. When they therefore were come together, they asked of him, saying, Lord, wilt thou at this time restore again the kingdom to Israel? And he said unto them, It is not for you to know the times or the seasons, which the Father hath put in his own power. **But ye shall receive power, after that the Holy Ghost is come upon you: and ye shall be witnesses unto me both in Jerusalem, and in all Judaea, and in Samaria, and unto the uttermost part of the earth.** And when he had spoken these things, while they beheld, he was taken up; and a cloud received him out of their sight.

*Wait in Jerusalem and you shall receive the Holy Ghost there. You will be a witness to me.

Mark 16:15-16 Jesus

 And he said unto them, Go ye into all the world, and preach the gospel to every creature. He that believeth and is **baptized shall be saved;** but he that **believeth not shall be damned.**

*There are many that will not accept what Jesus said here. In all the men of the Bible who has the greatest authority, Jesus.

Matthew 28:18-20

And Jesus came and spake unto them, saying, All power is given unto me in heaven and in earth. Go ye therefore, and teach all nations, baptizing them in the name of the Father, and of the Son, and of the Holy Ghost: **Teaching them to observe all things whatsoever I have commanded you:** and, lo, I am with you always, even unto the end of the world. Amen.

*Teach and observe all things.

Matthew 16:13

When Jesus came into the coasts of Caesarea Philippi, he asked his disciples, saying, Whom do men say that I the Son of man am? And they said, Some say that thou art John the Baptist: some, Elias; and others, Jeremias, or one of the prophets. He saith unto them, But whom say ye that I am? And Simon Peter answered and said, Thou art the Christ, the Son of the living God. And Jesus answered and said unto him, Blessed art thou, Simon Barjona: for flesh and blood hath not revealed it unto thee, but my Father which is in heaven. And I say also unto thee, That thou art Peter, and upon this rock **I will build my church;** and the gates of hell shall not prevail against it. And I will give unto thee the keys of the kingdom of heaven: and whatsoever thou shalt bind on earth shall be bound in heaven: and whatsoever thou shalt loose on earth shall be loosed in heaven.

*This is the first time Jesus mentions His Church. At this point in time the Church had not been establish. Many think the Church was built on Peter. But Jesus said my Church. The confusion is in words. (a.) Peter in the Greek, meaning a single stone - Petros. (b.) Rock, in the Greek, means a solid bed rock - Petra. These words in the Greek do mean the same.

1Corithians 10:4 Jesus the rock.

And did all drink the same spiritual drink: for they drank of that spiritual Rock that followed them: and that **Rock was Christ.**

*Mark 16:15: Jesus told His Apostles go into all the world and teach the Gospel. Let Paul define the Gospel.

1Corinthians 15:1-4 Gospel

Moreover, brethren, I declare unto you the gospel which I preached unto you, which also ye have received, and wherein ye stand; By which also ye are saved, if ye keep in memory what I preached unto you, unless ye have believed in vain. For I delivered unto you first of all that which I also received, how that **Christ died** for our sins according to the scriptures; And that he **was buried**, and that he **rose again** the third day according to the scriptures:

*The teaching of the Gospel is what draws mankind to Christ. The first time it was preached was in Acts 2:1-47. Remember teach and observe. If we are acceptable to these forty seven verses we will **duplicate** what these did on the day of Pentecost when they **heard the Gospel for the first time.** Now let us observe what went on.

Acts 2:1-47

And when the day of Pentecost was fully come, they were all with one accord in one place.

*This was fifty days after Jesus had ascended back to Heaven.

Verses 2-4

And suddenly there came a sound from heaven as of a rushing mighty wind, and it filled all the house where they were sitting. And there appeared unto them cloven tongues like as of fire, and it sat upon each of them. And they were all filled with the Holy Ghost, and began to speak with other tongues, as the Spirit gave them utterance.

*The Holy Spirit overwhelmed them with a gift so they would be able to convey the Gospel to all the Jewish languages that were present. The Apostles were unlearn in these languages by the standard of man.

Verses 5-11

And there were dwelling at Jerusalem Jews, devout men, out of every nation under heaven. Now when this was noised abroad, the multitude came together, and were confounded, **because that every man heard them speak in his own language.** And they were all amazed and marvelled, saying one to another, Behold, are not all these which speak Galilaeans? And how hear we every man in our own tongue, wherein we were born? Parthians, and Medes, and Elamites, and the dwellers in Mesopotamia, and in Judaea, and Cappadocia, in Pontus, and Asia, Phrygia, and Pamphylia, in Egypt, and in the parts of Libya about Cyrene, and strangers of Rome, Jews and proselytes, Cretes and Arabians, we do hear them speak in our tongues the wonderful works of God.

*All these people were able to hear and understand what was being taught, by the Apostles.

Verses 12-21

And they were all amazed, and were in doubt, saying one to another, What meaneth this? Others mocking said, These men are full of new wine. **But Peter, standing up with the eleven**, lifted up his voice, and said unto them, Ye men of Judaea, and all ye that dwell at Jerusalem, be this known unto you, and hearken to my words: For these are not drunken, as ye suppose, seeing it is but the third hour of the day. But this is that which was spoken by the prophet Joel; **And it shall come to pass in the last days**, saith God, I will pour out of my Spirit upon all flesh: and your sons and your daughters shall prophesy, and your young men shall see visions, and your old men shall dream dreams: And on my servants and on my handmaidens I will pour out in those days of my Spirit; and they shall prophesy: And I will shew wonders in heaven above, and signs in the earth beneath; blood, and fire, and vapour of smoke: The sun shall be turned into darkness, and the moon into blood, before the great and notable day of the Lord come: And it shall come to pass, that whosoever shall call on the name of the Lord shall be saved.

*The Apostles are letting them know that they knew of the Prophesy. They also knew the last days denote the last dispensation of Christ Jesus.

Verses 22-30

Ye men of Israel, hear these words; Jesus of Nazareth, a man approved of God among you by miracles and wonders and signs, which God did by him in the midst of you, as ye yourselves also know: Him, being delivered by the determinate counsel and foreknowledge of God, ye have taken, and by wicked hands have crucified and slain: Whom God hath raised up, having loosed the pains of death: because it was not possible that he should be holden of it.

For David speaketh concerning him, I foresaw the Lord always before my face, for he is on my right hand, that I should not be moved: Therefore did my heart rejoice, and my tongue was glad; moreover also my flesh shall rest in hope: Because thou wilt not leave my soul in hell, neither wilt thou suffer thine Holy One to see corruption. Thou hast made known to me the ways of life; thou shalt make me full of joy with thy countenance. Men and brethren, let me freely speak unto you of the patriarch David, that he is both dead and buried, and his sepulchre is with us unto this day. Therefore being a prophet, and knowing that God had sworn with an oath to him, that of the fruit of his loins, according to the flesh, **he would raise up Christ to sit on his throne;**

*The problem with the Jews, they continued to believe this throne of David would be an earthly kingdom. But you will see later in this chapter it is the church. A spiritual kingdom.

Verses 31-35

He seeing this before spake of the resurrection of Christ, that his soul was not left in hell, neither his flesh did see corruption. This Jesus hath God raised up, whereof we all are witnesses. Therefore being by the right hand of God exalted, and having received of the Father the promise of the Holy Ghost, he hath shed forth this, which ye now see and hear. For David is not ascended into the heavens: but he saith himself, The Lord said unto my Lord, Sit thou on my right hand, Until I make thy foes thy footstool.

*What you see and hear is the promise from God.

Verses 36

Therefore let all the house of Israel know assuredly, that God hath made the same Jesus, whom ye have crucified, both Lord and Christ.

*Food for thought: We are no different than the Jews on Pentecost because from day of accountability of our lives, until now if we has not done what God expects of us we are crucifying Christ afresh. (Romans 3:23 - For all have sinned, and come short of the glory of God).

Verses 37-38

Now when they heard this, they were pricked in their heart, and said unto Peter and to the rest of the apostles, Men and brethren, what shall we do? Then Peter said unto them, Repent, and be baptized every one of you in the name of Jesus Christ for the remission of sins, and ye shall receive the gift of the Holy Ghost.

*When the Jews heard they had crucified their savior, they repented and wanted to know how to get rid of this sin. Listen to what was told of them. Be baptized in the name of Jesus Christ for remission of this sin. Remission - an act of forgiving.

Verse 39

For the promise is unto you, and to your children, and to all that are **afar off**, even as many as the LORD our God shall call.

*Afar off – Gentiles. God's promise to Abraham (Genesis 12:3- And I will bless them that bless thee, and curse him that curseth thee: and in thee shall **all families of the earth be blessed**.)

Verses 40-47

67

And with many other words did he testify and exhort, saying, Save yourselves from this untoward generation. **Then they that gladly received his word were baptized**: and the same day there were **added** unto them about three thousand souls. And they continued stedfastly in the apostles' doctrine and fellowship, and in breaking of bread, and in prayers. And fear came upon every soul: and many wonders and signs were done by the apostles. And all that believed were together, and had all things common; And sold their possessions and goods, and parted them to all men, as every man had need. And they, continuing daily with one accord in the temple, and breaking bread from house to house, did eat their meat with gladness and singleness of heart, Praising God, and having favour with all the people. **And the Lord added to the church daily such as should be saved.**

*Notice: The Lord added the saved to His Church. There is no voting to get into Jesus Church. What you vote in you can vote out. Can you identify your church in the Bible?

Let us take a look at few other conversions to Jesus Doctrine.

Acts 8:26-39 Ethiopian Eunuch

And the angel of the Lord spake unto Philip, saying, Arise, and go toward the south unto the way that goeth down from Jerusalem unto Gaza, which is desert. And he arose and went: and, behold, a man of Ethiopia, an eunuch of great authority under Candace queen of the Ethiopians, who had the charge of all her treasure, and had come to Jerusalem for to worship, Was returning, and sitting in his chariot read Esaias the prophet. Then the Spirit said unto Philip, Go near, and join thyself to this chariot. **And Philip ran thither to him, and heard him read the prophet Esaias, and said, Understandest thou what thou readest?** And he said, How can I, except some man should guide me? And he desired Philip that he would come up and sit with him. **The place of the scripture** which he read was this, He was led as a sheep to the slaughter; and like a lamb dumb before his shearer, so opened he not his mouth: In his humiliation his judgment was taken away: and who shall declare his generation? for his life is taken from the earth.

*Verses 32-33 reference to (Isaiah 53:1-12).

And the eunuch answered Philip, and said, I pray thee, of whom speaketh the prophet this? of himself, or of some other man? Then Philip opened his mouth, and began at the same scripture, and **preached unto him Jesus.** And as they went on their way, they **came unto a certain water: and the eunuch said, See, here is water; what doth hinder me to be baptized?** And Philip said, If thou believest with all thine heart, thou mayest. And he answered and said, I believe that Jesus Christ is the Son of God. And he commanded the chariot to stand still: **and they went down both into the water, both Philip and the eunuch; and he baptized him.** And when they were come up out of the water, the Spirit of the Lord caught away Philip, that the eunuch saw him no more: and he went on his way rejoicing.

*Verse 35 Philip preached unto him Jesus. Notice Philip did not say anything about water. The Eunuch bought up water and wanted to be baptized. There has to be a reason for this.

Reason, Listen to Paul: Romans 6:3-8

What shall we say then? Shall we continue in sin, that grace may abound? God forbid. How shall we, that are dead to sin, live any longer therein? Know ye not, that so many of us as were baptized into Jesus Christ were baptized into his death? Therefore we are buried with him by baptism into death: that like as Christ was raised up from the dead by the glory of the Father, even so we also should walk in newness of life. For if we have been planted together in the likeness of his death, we shall be also in the likeness of his resurrection: Knowing this, that our old man is crucified with him, that the body of sin might be destroyed, that henceforth we should not serve sin. For he that is dead is freed from sin.

Now if we be dead with Christ, we believe that we shall also live with him:

Let us take a look at another conversion.

Acts 10:1-48 Cornelius a Gentile

There was a certain man in Caesarea called Cornelius, a centurion of the band called the Italian band, A devout man, and **one that feared God with all his house,** which gave much alms to the people, and prayed to God alway. He saw in a vision evidently about the ninth hour of the day an angel of God coming in to him, and saying unto him, Cornelius. And when he looked on him, he was afraid, and said, What is it, Lord? And he said unto him, Thy prayers and thine alms are come up for a memorial before God. And now **send men to Joppa, and call for one Simon, whose surname is Peter:** He lodgeth with one Simon a tanner, whose house is by the sea side: **he shall tell thee what thou oughtest to do.** And when the angel which spake unto Cornelius was departed, he called two of his household servants, and a devout soldier of them that waited on him continually; And when he had declared all these things unto them, **he sent them to Joppa.** On the morrow, as they went on their journey, and drew nigh unto the city, Peter went up upon the housetop to pray about the sixth hour: And he became very hungry, and would have eaten: but while they made ready, he fell into a trance, And saw heaven opened, and a certain vessel descending upon him, as it had been a great sheet knit at the four corners, and let down to the earth: Wherein were all manner of fourfooted beasts of the earth, and wild beasts, and creeping things, and fowls of the air. And there came a voice to him, Rise, Peter; kill, and eat. But Peter said, Not so, Lord; for I have never eaten any thing that is common or unclean. And the voice spake unto him again the second time, What God hath cleansed, that call not thou common.

This was done thrice: and the vessel was received up again into heaven. Now while Peter doubted in himself what this vision which he had seen should mean, behold, the men which were sent from Cornelius had made enquiry for Simon's house, and stood before the gate, And called, and asked whether Simon, which was surnamed Peter, were lodged there. While Peter thought on the vision, the Spirit said unto him, Behold, three men seek thee. Arise therefore, and get thee down, and go with them, doubting nothing: for I have sent them. Then Peter went down to the men which were sent unto him from Cornelius; and said, Behold, I am he whom ye seek: what is the cause wherefore ye are come? **And they said, Cornelius the centurion, a just man, and one that feareth God, and of good report among all the nation of the Jews, was warned from God by an holy angel to send for thee into his house, and to hear words of thee.** Then called he them in, and lodged them. And on the morrow Peter went away with them, and certain brethren from Joppa accompanied him. And the morrow after they entered into Caesarea. And Cornelius waited for them, and he had called together his kinsmen and near friends. **And as Peter was coming in, Cornelius met him, and fell down at his feet, and worshipped him. But Peter took him up, saying, Stand up; I myself also am a man.** And as he talked with him, he went in, and found many that were come together. And he said unto them, **Ye know how that it is an unlawful thing for a man that is a Jew to keep company, or come unto one of another nation; but God hath shewed me that I should not call any man common or unclean.** Therefore came I unto you without gainsaying, as soon as I was sent for: I ask therefore for what intent ye have sent for me? And Cornelius said, Four days ago I was fasting until this hour; and at the ninth hour I prayed in my house, and, behold, a man stood before me in bright clothing, And said, Cornelius, thy prayer is heard, and thine alms are had in remembrance in the sight of God.

Send therefore to Joppa, and call hither Simon, whose surname is Peter; he is lodged in the house of one Simon a tanner by the sea side: who, when he cometh, shall speak unto thee. Immediately therefore I sent to thee; and thou hast well done that thou art come. Now therefore are we all here present before God, to hear all things that are commanded thee of God. **Then Peter opened his mouth, and said, Of a truth I perceive that God is no respecter of persons:** But in every nation he that feareth him, and worketh righteousness, is accepted with him. The word which God sent unto the children of Israel, preaching peace by Jesus Christ: (he is Lord of all:) That word, I say, ye know, which was published throughout all Judaea, and began from Galilee, after the baptism which John preached; How God anointed Jesus of Nazareth with the Holy Ghost and with power: who went about doing good, and healing all that were oppressed of the devil; for God was with him. And we are witnesses of all things which he did both in the land of the Jews, and in Jerusalem; whom they slew and hanged on a tree: Him God raised up the third day, and shewed him openly; Not to all the people, but unto witnesses chosen before God, even to us, who did eat and drink with him after he rose from the dead. And he commanded us to preach unto the people, and to testify that it is he which was ordained of God to be the Judge of quick and dead. To him give all the prophets witness, that through his name whosoever believeth in him shall receive remission of sins. **While Peter yet spake these words, the Holy Ghost fell on all them which heard the word. And they of the circumcision which believed were astonished, as many as came with Peter, because that on the Gentiles also was poured out the gift of the Holy Ghost. For they heard them speak with tongues, and magnify God. Then answered Peter,**

*Reference: Acts 2:2-4 The day of Pentecost.

Can any man forbid water, that these should not be baptized, which have received the Holy Ghost as well as we?

And **he commanded them to be baptized in the name of the Lord.** Then prayed they him to tarry certain days.

*Cornelius and his household were baptized.

Acts 16:16-34 The Jailer

And it came to pass, as we went to prayer, a certain damsel possessed with a spirit of divination met us, which brought her masters much gain by soothsaying: The same followed Paul and us, and cried, saying, These men are the servants of the most high God, which shew unto us the way of salvation. And this did she many days. But Paul, being grieved, turned and said to the spirit, I command thee in the name of Jesus Christ to come out of her. And he came out the same hour. **And when her masters saw that the hope of their gains was gone, they caught Paul and Silas, and drew them into the marketplace unto the rulers,** And brought them to the magistrates, saying, These men, being Jews, do exceedingly trouble our city, **And teach customs, which are not lawful for us to receive, neither to observe, being Romans.** And the multitude rose up together against them: and the magistrates rent off their clothes, and commanded to beat them. **And when they had laid many stripes upon them, they cast them into prison, charging the jailor to keep them safely:** Who, having received such a charge, thrust them into the inner prison, and made their feet fast in the stocks. **And at midnight Paul and Silas prayed, and sang praises unto God: and the prisoners heard them.** And suddenly there was a great earthquake, so that the foundations of the prison were shaken: and immediately all the doors were opened, and every one's bands were loosed. And the keeper of the prison awaking out of his sleep, and seeing the prison doors open, **he drew out his sword, and would have killed himself,** supposing that the prisoners had been fled.

But Paul cried with a loud voice, saying, Do thyself no harm: for we are all here. Then he called for a light, and sprang in, and came trembling, and fell down before Paul and Silas, **And brought them out, and said, Sirs, what must I do to be saved?** And they said, **Believe on the Lord Jesus Christ, and thou shalt be saved,** and thy house.

*Many take what Paul says here, believe and thou shalt be saved out of context. This jailer did not know the things Paul and Silas knew, because this religion being taught was new. The answer to the jailer's question, you have to believe on Jesus and His doctrine to be saved. Faith is the first step toward salvation.

And they spoke unto him the word of the Lord, and to all that were in his house.

*Paul and Silas spoke the Gospel to all that were in the jailer house.

And he took them the same hour of the night, and washed their stripes; and was baptized, he and all his, straightway.

*The jailer took Paul and Silas the same hour, nursed and washed their stripes. Than the jailer and all his household were baptized.

And when he had brought them into his house, he set meat before them, and rejoiced, believing in God with all his house.

CAN YOU IDENTIFY YOUR CHURCH IN THE BIBLE?

74

Please do not take my word for what is written in this book. Take your Bible and make sure for yourself. Because you will at the end of life stand before God alone.

According to Acts 2:38

Then Peter said unto them, Repent, and be baptized every one of you in the name of Jesus Christ for the remission of sins, and ye shall receive the gift of the Holy Ghost.

*Repent - turn from sin, be regretful.

Remission - act of being forgiven.

Acts 2:47

Praising God, and having favour with all the people. **And the Lord added to the church daily such as should be saved.**

*Baptism and the Church go hand a hand. The Lord adds the Baptized to His Church.

1Peter 3:20-21 Baptism Saves

Which sometime were disobedient, when once the longsuffering of God waited in the days of Noah, while the ark was a preparing, wherein few, that is, **eight souls were saved by water. The like figure whereunto even baptism doth also now save us** (not the putting away of the filth of the flesh, but the answer of a good conscience toward God,) by the resurrection of Jesus Christ:

*There is a lot of controversy on the word baptize. Baptize is a word that was never translated into the English language. I am going to let you find the meaning for yourself. Start with these two words: The Greek word Baptizo and Baptisma. I could give you the answer, but I am not going to. To find the meaning you will understand Jesus baptism for us. If you have not accepted it as of now. Remember, I promise not to be giving my opinion. That why I want you to study all these scriptures for yourself in this book.

*There are many things that have been taught to us over the years. But we never have investigated to see if they are true.

Matthew 7:7-8 Listen to Jesus

Ask, and it shall be given you; seek, and ye shall find; knock, and it shall be opened unto you: For every one that asketh receiveth; and he that seeketh findeth; and to him that knocketh it shall be opened.

Proverbs 16:25

There is a way that seemeth right unto a man, but the end thereof are the ways of death.

*There are five steps to become a member of the Church of Christ. It takes all five to be in harmony with God's word. Four are a mindset and one is an action, and all five leads to salvation.

Mark 16:15-16 Jesus Baptism

And he said unto them, Go ye into all the world, and preach the gospel to every creature. **He that believeth and is baptized shall be saved;** but he that believeth not shall be damned.

*But whoever will not believe the gospel will be condemned. There are many people that confess Christ Jesus that will not accept this statement. This is a direct command of Jesus. All you have to do is reverse the statement and you will see what He mean.

To become a member of the Christ Jesus Church.

1.**Hear** - to perceive with the ear.

Romans 10:17 So then faith cometh by hearing, and hearing by the word of God.

2. **Believe** – to regard as true; to trust; to have faith.

Hebrew 11:6 But without faith it is impossible to please him: for he that cometh to God must believe that he is, and that he is a rewarder of them that diligently seek him.

3. **Repent -** to regret for a deed; to change one's life of sin.

Luke 13:3 I tell you, Nay: but, except ye repent, ye shall all likewise perish.

4. **Confession**- to acknowledge. (Jesus is the Son of God).

Romans 10:10 For with the heart man believeth unto righteousness; and with the mouth confession is made unto salvation.

5. **Baptize**- a burial (submerge in water)

Acts 2:38 Then Peter said unto them, Repent, and be **baptized** every one of you in the name of Jesus Christ for **the remission of sins,** and ye shall receive the gift of the Holy Ghost.

*Food for thought - Buried. I believe we all can agree Jesus died, was buried and rose from the dead. We just duplicate His burial in water.

Romans 6:3-4 Know ye not, that so many of us as were baptized into Jesus Christ were baptized into his death? Therefore we are **buried with him by baptism into death**: that like as Christ was raised up from the dead by the glory of the Father, **even so we also should walk in newness of life.**

*Once the Lord adds us to His Church, there is an order of Worship in His Church in which we should take a part in every first day of the week - Sunday.

Hebrews 10:25-26

Not forsaking the assembling of ourselves together, as the manner of some is; but exhorting one another: and so much the more, as ye see the day approaching. For if we sin wilfully after that we have received the knowledge of the truth, there remaineth no more sacrifice for sins,

Items of Worship

The Jews had a Holy Day in the Old Testament.

Exodus 20:8-11 The Sabbath, Saturday.

Remember the sabbath day, to keep it holy. Six days shalt thou labour, and do all thy work: But the **seventh day is the sabbath** of the LORD thy God: in it thou shalt not do any work, thou, nor thy son, nor thy daughter, thy manservant, nor thy maidservant, nor thy cattle, nor thy stranger that is within thy gates: For in six days the LORD made heaven and earth, the sea, and all that in them is, **and rested the seventh day:** wherefore the LORD blessed the **sabbath day, and hallowed it.**

*The Christian or the followers of Christ Jesus has a day. The first day of the week, Sunday. There are five items of worship practiced in - The New Testament. The Lord's memorial supper, Preaching, prayer, giving of money, singing without the use mechanical instruments. John 4:24, God is a Spirit: and they that worship him must worship him in spirit and in truth.

1. **Jesus Memorial Supper**

Acts 20:7 Every first day of the week-Sunday.

And upon the first day of the week, when the disciples came together to break bread, Paul preached unto them, ready to depart on the morrow; and continued his speech until midnight.

1Corinthians 11:23-26 Purpose for the breaking of beard.

For I have received of the Lord that which also I delivered unto you, that the Lord Jesus the same night in which he was betrayed took bread: And when he had given thanks, he brake it, and said, Take, eat: this is my body, which is broken for you: this do in remembrance of me. After the same manner also he took the cup, when he had supped, saying, this cup is the new testament in my blood: this do ye, as oft as ye drink it, in remembrance of me. For as often as ye eat this bread, and drink this cup, ye do shew the Lord's death till he come.

2. **Singing-without the use of mechanical instruments.**

Ephesians 5:19

Speaking to yourselves in psalms and hymns and spiritual songs, singing and making melody in your heart to the Lord;

Colossians 3:16

Let the word of Christ dwell in you richly in all wisdom; teaching and admonishing one another in psalms and hymns and spiritual songs, singing with grace in your hearts to the Lord.

Hebrews 13:15 Fruit of our lips-A'cappella.

By him therefore let us offer the sacrifice of praise to God continually, that is, the **fruit of our lips giving thanks to his name.**

*I know many try to keep the things David did. But David was not under the doctrine of Christ Jesus. So Psalms 100, 150 and other scripture of The Old Testament cannot justify having mechanical instruments in the Lord's Church of the New Testament Age.

3. **Their Offering was given on the first day of the week-Sunday.**

1Corinthians 16:1-2

Now concerning the collection for the saints, as I have given order to the churches of Galatia, even so do ye. Upon the first day of the week let every one of you lay by him in store, as God hath prospered him, that there be no gatherings when I come.

*I believe you cannot find any church in which they do not take up an offering on Sunday. If can take up an offering why omit the Lord's Supper on Sunday.

4. **Bible Study and Prayer.**

Acts 20:7

And upon the first day of the week, when the disciples came together to break bread, Paul **preached unto them**, ready to depart on the morrow; and continued his speech until midnight.

1Thessalonians 5:17

Pray without ceasing.

5. **Singing-fruit of the lips.**

Ephesians 5:19

 Speaking to yourselves in psalms and hymns and spiritual songs, singing and making melody in your heart to the Lord;

*If you study your Bible you will see the need to observe these items of worship every first day of the week-Sunday.

Conclusion

Can you identify your church in the Bible? After reading this book and your church cannot be identified in the Bible or by this book, you need to do the more research.

Some identifying features that is not a part of the Lord's Church.

Psalms 111:9

He sent redemption unto his people: he hath commanded his covenant for ever: holy and **reverend is his name.**

***Reverend is God's name** and man should not be call by this name.

Matthew 23:9-10

 And **call no man your father upon the earth:** for one is your Father, which is in heaven. Neither be ye called masters: for one is your Master, even Christ.

*Call no man father or master from a **religious stand-point** in the church.

1Corinthians 14:33-35

For God is not the author of confusion, but of peace, as in all churches of the saints. **Let your women keep silence in the churches:** for it is not permitted unto them to speak; but they are commanded to be under obedience as also saith the law. **And if they will learn any thing,** let them **ask their husbands at home:** for it is a shame for women to speak in the church.

1Timothy 2:11-12

Let the woman learn in silence with all subjection. But I suffer not a woman to teach, **nor to usurp authority over the man**, but to be in silence.

1Peter 3:1

Likewise, ye wives, be in subjection to your own husbands; that, if any obey not the word, they also may without the word be won by the conversation of the wives;

*Many man made doctrines turn a deaf ear to these scriptures allowing women to preach.

1Corinthians 14:21

In the law it is written, With men of other tongues and other lips will I speak unto this people; and **yet for all that will they not hear me, saith the Lord.**

James 2:10

For whosoever shall keep the whole law, and **yet offend in one point, he is guilty of all.**

*I have studied with many people over the years. Very few I have studied with accepts God's word at face value. It saddens me, because I know with everyone I have studied with that rejected God's word. I have sealed their fate, they will have no excuse when they stand before God at judgment. No matter what we feel, believe or think. God word will never change.

Isaiah 55:6 -11

Seek ye the LORD while he may be found, call ye upon him while he is near: Let the wicked forsake his way, and the unrighteous man his thoughts: and let him return unto the LORD, and he will have mercy upon him; and to our God, for he will abundantly pardon. **For my thoughts are not your thoughts, neither are your ways my ways, saith the LORD.** For as the heavens are higher than the earth, so are my ways higher than your ways, and my thoughts than your thoughts. For as the rain cometh down, and the snow from heaven, and returneth not thither, but watereth the earth, and maketh it bring forth and bud, that it may give seed to the sower, and bread to the eater: **So shall my word be that goeth forth out of my mouth: it shall not return unto me void,** but it shall accomplish that which I please, and it shall prosper in the thing whereto I sent it.

Matthew 7:21-27

Not every one that saith unto me, Lord, Lord, shall enter into the kingdom of heaven; but he that doeth the will of my Father which is in heaven. Many will say to me in that day, Lord, Lord, have we not prophesied in thy name? and in thy name have cast out devils? and in thy name done many wonderful works? And then will I profess unto them, I never knew you: depart from me, ye that work iniquity. Therefore whosoever heareth these sayings of mine, and doeth them, I will liken him unto a wise man, which built his house upon a rock: And the rain descended, and the floods came, and the winds blew, and beat upon that house; and it fell not: for it was founded upon a rock. And every one that heareth these sayings of mine, and doeth them not, shall be likened unto a foolish man, which built his house upon the sand: And the rain descended, and the floods came, and the winds blew, and beat upon that house; and it fell: and great was the fall of it.

*I hope these scripture will help you find your way into salvation.

In the name of "The Father, The Son and The Holy Ghost Amen.